# "L.U.C.K.Y." MARRIAGES DON'T JUST HAPPEN!

## HOW TO HAVE A "LUCKY" MARRIAGE HANDBOOK

By Judy Siracusa

Published by
USA United Publishing
1212 4th Avenue SW
Largo, FL 33770

ISBN: 0-9708837-0-6

san number  253-7346

Library of Congress Control Number 2001012345

Some of the names and identifying details in this book have been changed.

---

# DEDICATION

To my best friend, Pat,

for all the love and support

he has always given me.

**"L.U.C.K.Y." Marriages  Don't Just Happen**

## ACKNOWLEDGMENTS

Thanks to all my family and friends who encouraged me to complete my book. The idea of writing a positive, up-beat book about marriage has long been in my mind and heart. The problem I faced was that I am a speaker, not a writer. Through uplifting support and guidance I have managed to produce this book on marriage that I hope will help others achieve some of the successes that my "lucky" couples have achieved in their marriages.

Thanks to my daughter-in-law, Kara, the first to look at my beginning ideas—and not reject them. Thanks to my son, David, the next family member to review, comment on, and approve my project. Thanks also to my son, Brian, still single (quite handsome, bright, and athletic, I might add!) who amazed me by reading my book on marriage in the back seat of the car while riding to the Southeast Conference championship football game in Atlanta. His enjoyment of the book was not only a surprise, but also real encouragement! And, thanks to my brother, Vince, whose fine-tuning of my writing is much appreciated.

A very special thanks to my patient friend, Jim Tucker.

Thanks also to my dear friends, Claudia Lynn and Sue Schott.

Harriet Coren, part of one of the "lucky" couples in the book, you were truly the final push I needed to complete my project. You took my book ideas home, read them, and then called the next day to say, "You must do it!" It was then that I knew it would get done. Harriet is a "D." When you finish reading this book you will understand what I mean.

Thanks last, but far from least, to my husband, Pat, who has listened and listened and listened!

# TABLE OF CONTENTS

As a professional member of the National Speakers Association, I travel around the country working with corporate clients in a wide variety of industries. All of my training is based on "people skills"—sales, customer service, team building, management, communications, stress, and time management. Each industry is unique, but the need for "people skills" is universal.

My programs are based upon behavioral styles. Whether presenting communications, stress, management, or team building I always incorporate behavioral styles into my presentations. I emphasize that we are all different from each other. Because of this our needs and the needs of our customers, clients, and staff are all different and must be dealt with in different ways. The behavioral styles are based upon the DISC Personal Profile System. The DISC styles help people understand themselves and others. They are excellent training tools.

The DISC Personal Profile System teaches people to recognize and work more effectively with different behavioral styles. Over the years I have been amazed that wherever I go and to whatever group I am presenting there is always a common bond in the questions asked of me. The questions are about behavioral styles, not how they relate to business, but how they relate to their personal lives. Improving their personal relationships is what interests most people!

"What style would make the best mate for me?" "Why do my spouse and I have such conflict?" "Why was I so attracted to my spouse's style before we were married and now that same style drives me crazy?" "Can you tell which styles would get along best?" I train people about customer, client, and employee relationships, but their major concerns are about personal relationships—love, compatibility, and marriage!

Behavioral Style training is very effective in the business arena. My business, WINNING WAYS of Tampa Bay, Inc., has successfully focused on this area for more than seven years. Through the years I have found it as effective as it relates to personal relationships.

Marriage is one of the most life-altering relationships an individual can ever enter into. Deciding to marry, who to marry, and when to marry are all huge life changing choices. Marriage can be, is, and has been for many, the very worst institution. Yet, marriage should be and can be the most incredibly wonderful institution!

I cherish a strong marriage with all my heart! Being married to my best friend, having a lifetime commitment with the person I like, love, and care for more than anyone in the whole world is truly wonderful. Our marriage, our unconditional love, and our enjoyment of each other have filled us with an incredible spirit for over 35 years! People often comment on the success of our marriage. Family, friends, even acquaintances frequently comment, "You two are so lucky!"

Personal relationship questions posed during breaks, comments about my "lucky" marriage, and all the publicity and attention given to unhappy marriages and divorces has prompted me to write, *"L.U.C.K.Y." Marriages Don't Just Happen! How To Have a "Lucky" Marriage Handbook.*

So much time is devoted to the negative side of marriage in articles, books, and on talk shows. It is time to focus on the positive aspects of successful marriages and to take a look at just what contributes to "lucky" marriages.

Yes, my husband, Pat, and I have been "lucky." Many other couples are "lucky" too. There are reasons for this luck! I will share experiences and life stories from our marriage as well as the experiences and life stories of three other very "lucky" couples. These will be used to define, explain, and emphasize some of the points made in each of the areas of a "L.U.C.K.Y." marriage. The couples whose stories are included in this book have very different backgrounds, very different behavioral styles, and very different marriages, yet each possesses important qualities and beliefs presented in this handbook. They have successfully established their own unique, "lucky" marriages.

One other couple's experiences and stories are also included in the book. Unfortunately, at this point in time, this couple's marriage can not be considered a "lucky" marriage, rather just a "surviving" marriage. They are still married, but they are struggling. They are included to emphasize some of my concerns with relationship issues in marriage. Initially I considered using them as one of the "lucky" couples. However, the more I observed, the more I interviewed, and the more they shared, the more concerned I became about the future strength of their marriage.  They have many wonderful qualities that could have contributed to a very successful marriage, and hopefully still can, but along the way some very important ingredients have been neglected.  Presently they are in counseling.

Is there such a thing as a perfect marriage?  Is there a perfect life?  Challenges are inevitable in marriage as in life.  Handling things in a union of love and commitment with a partner of the same spirit makes them exactly that— marriage and life challenges— not marriage and life tragedies.

I believe strongly in the strength and the beauty of marriage.  Pat and I have been so fortunate in our marriage as have the other three couples represented.  It is because I want to help others experience a "lucky" marriage that I have written this book.  It will help young people thinking about marriage, as well as older people contemplating a second, third, or even fourth marriage, to understand the basic ingredients of a "lucky" marriage.  "Lucky" marriages do not just happen.  There are reasons why marriages are "lucky."

This handbook is simple and to the point.  It is an important read for married couples whose marriages are "functioning" but would not be considered "lucky."  And, it is a "must read" before entering into the institution of marriage—an institution which can be the WORST...OR THE BEST!

## CHAPTER ONE

## "L"

### "L" Stands for Like

The "L" in a "L.U.C.K.Y." marriage is not only the first letter, but also perhaps one of the most important ingredients in a "L.U.C.K.Y." marriage. The "L" does not stand for LOVE! Love is wonderful. Love is special. Love is important. But love is not nearly as important as the first most important ingredient in a "L.U.C.K.Y." marriage: Like!

Like each other! Liking each other sounds so basic, so simple—a no-brainer! However, as basic as it is, it is probably the most overlooked ingredient contributing to the many unsuccessful marriages. It is simple, basic, and so very important.

❀❀❀ *Like your spouse* ❀❀❀

Why would you marry a person you do not like? We would not choose someone to be our friend we do not like. At work, in school, or socially, we try to avoid people we do not like. Yet, so many marry people they do not like.

Think about spending a lifetime with someone you do not like. Why would anyone do this to himself or herself? People do it for a number of reasons. They may be infatuated and totally enthralled with the person, unable to get through the

1

infatuation to see the basic person who, in fact, they do not like. It may also be the looks, the charm, or the sex. Sometimes it is the other person's status, wealth, or position in the community.  The individual may not see, or in some cases, may not choose to see beyond the infatuation—the passion of the moment or the pressure of the situation.

It may be the pressure put on the future spouse to say, "Yes."  Or, it may be the pressure put upon them by the people around them.  Some may feel it is the time to get married or worse yet, time may be running out for them! Even though this may not be the perfect match, or even a good match, this one <u>must</u> do.

Others, I believe, may get caught up in the infatuation of a wedding. They are simply and completely overwhelmed with the idea of the WEDDING.  The BIG DAY!  They want the perfect wedding—the wedding they have dreamed and planned for all of their lives.  To do this, one needs to have a person to marry.  It is possible, I think, to make someone into the person you need them to be for a certain period of time—perhaps even long enough to have the perfect wedding.  But, unless you like this person, you will certainly not have a perfect marriage, or even a good or lasting one!

Others perhaps convince themselves that although they do not truly like the person, they love the person so much that things will work out.  I have heard people say, "I think I love him or her, but I am not sure if I like him or her!"  Love conquers all only in fairy tales.

So many individuals enter the institution of marriage with the misconception that they can change their spouse. It is a huge mistake to enter marriage with the idea that you can change your spouse to make him or her into the person you want them to be. I have heard young people planning to marry say, "I am so in love! I am not saying I like everything about my future spouse, but I will change those things I dislike once we are married." Do not plan on changing your spouse.

*❀❀❀ You cannot change your spouse*
*to fit your mold ❀❀❀*

## LIKE vs. LOVE

Before Pat and I married, my mom freely shared her negative feelings about marriage. My mom, although a very caring person, is also a very cautious and critical one. Time and again she would tell me that everyone thought their marriage was going to be different, but that they all ended the same—mundane and frustrating! At the same time, she always cautioned me to marry someone I liked. She said, "When the thrill and the romance is gone (and it will be) you might as well be left with someone you like." I followed her advice and married someone that I liked.

She was wrong, however, about our marriage turning into a mundane and frustrating existence. Thanks, Mom, your cautioning advice helped contribute to a lifetime of happiness!

There is a much greater chance of success in marriage if there is "like" without love, than if there is love without "like." A marriage without like does not have a chance to be a "lucky" marriage. Like can slowly grow into love over a period of time. But, love without like will grow into dislike! What we do not like at the beginning of a relationship, we <u>hate</u> after the wedding.

*❀❀❀ Like lasts!*
*Love without like turns into dislike ❀❀❀*

I am not saying that people do not change and evolve. They do. However, they do not change and evolve by the plan of another. We all learn and grow through the years, but I think our basic character remains the same.

*❀❀❀ Do not plan on changing your spouse*
*after the wedding ❀❀❀*

There is a common expression, "Look at your future spouse's mother or father and you will know what your spouse will look like in 20 to 30 years." <u>More</u> <u>importantly,</u> take a good look at how your future spouse's parents treat each other. Take a good look, also, at how your future spouse treats his or her parents, siblings, and friends. These are strong indicators of how your spouse will treat you in future years. The relationship is different, but I believe the treatment will be basically the same.

*❀❀❀ Look at how your future spouse*
*treats family and friends ❀❀❀*

I am not suggesting that you must search for perfection in a mate. Perfection probably does not exist. You should select a mate, first and foremost, that you basically like. Once you make a decision, be able to accept this mate as he or she is. Your spouse should have many wonderful qualities you admire and like and probably a few that you do not. Choose a spouse with many positives and a few negatives. Be realistic. No one is faultless. Do not build expectations that are impossible to meet; instead look for what is most important. Find a mate whose faults you can accept. Liking is very important. Can there be a perfect person? No! Yet, I believe, there can be a perfect mate. A perfect mate is one you like, respect, and care for, and who, in turn, likes, respects, and cares for you.

> ❁❁❁ *There are no perfect individuals,*
> *but there can be a perfect spouse* ❁❁❁

There is no greater source of strength for growth of character and achievement than receiving unconditional liking and loving from another person. Being appreciated and affirmed adds untold amounts of self-esteem and belief in oneself. This kind of support will add to each spouse's strengths and will foster continued development throughout a lifetime.

> ❁❁❁ *Liking and loving can add so much to the*
> *positive development of each spouse* ❁❁❁

Pat and I have done so much for each other in our growth as individuals. We like and enjoy each other—always have. He likes and loves me so much he makes me like and love myself! He makes me feel special because he thinks I am attractive, fun, a good athlete, a caring person, a good dancer and, most importantly, a good wife and mother. I believe I make him feel the same way because I think he is handsome, intelligent, a great athlete, a kind, considerate person, a good dancer, and a wonderful husband and father. One of his most special qualities is his incredibly positive attitude toward life! His zest for life is surpassed by none! Am I perfect? Is Pat perfect? No. But, for me, Pat is a perfect mate. He may not be a perfect human being, and he may not be a perfect mate for someone else, but he is perfect for me.

We have come to a place in our lives we could not have even dreamed about when we met 39 years ago . . .

## 🍀 Pat and Judy Siracusa

Pat and I met the first week of college. We were both Physical Education Majors at the State University of New York, College at Cortland. It was friendship at first sight! We dated all four years and married two weeks after graduation. We both came from lower middle class Italian families. He was from Buffalo, New York; I was from Westchester, New York. Pat was the first in his family to attend college. In my family there were a few college graduates before me. Getting college degrees and becoming teachers was considered a high level of success in both our families.

We graduated and started teaching in Poughkeepsie, New York. We bought a home in a nice family neighborhood one year after marrying. My parents never owned a home, so buying one was one of my early goals.

I retired from teaching full-time after three years to become a full-time mom. That is what we did back in the 60's. Pat taught a number of years before we returned to Cortland so he could attend graduate school. We had one son at the time. We struggled to make ends meet, but we both understood the value of education.

After returning to our home in Poughkeepsie, Pat continued to teach and coach high school basketball and tennis. He was a wonderful teacher and a wonderful coach. As a self-taught tennis player, he had become good enough to play number two on our college tennis team. In the late 60's and the early 70's tennis was at its peak. Pat took advantage of the market and began giving tennis lessons and clinics in his free time. Due to his natural ability with people, he built quite a tennis business. Financially, it became more lucrative than teaching high school.

So in the summer of 1974 we decided to chase a dream—warm weather, tennis and a totally different lifestyle. We packed up our three sons, ages one, three, and six, and headed to Florida. We had no jobs, no permanent place to stay, and only $2,000 in our savings account!

What made us have the guts to do this? We believed in ourselves and our ability to survive—for at least one year. Pat was on a one-year leave of absence. I had already left a two-year part-time teaching position at Marist College to have our third son.

Not only did we survive; we had a wonderful time and chose not to return north. We loved the sunshine, the people, and our new life in Clearwater, Florida.

After a few weeks of searching, Pat obtained a position in a country club as the sole tennis pro. We were given an apartment to live in and full profit from all the lessons Pat could teach. A great deal, huh?

Well, there were a few major drawbacks. East Bay Country Club was not a tennis club; it was a golf club. There were two crumbling tennis courts, no pro shop, and no tennis members!

Pat did everything possible to build the tennis membership. Again, his positive attitude and his natural ability to relate to people helped him as he went out to local public courts and met people to bring to East Bay Country Club. He knew if he could get just one person to take a lesson things would start to happen. Jackie Rice was his lesson and it started to happen!

He got the club to build just two more tennis courts and a very, very tiny pro shop. Four people in the shop and it became a fire hazard! That was the way the six-and-a-half years of being a tennis pro began. By the time Pat left East Bay Country Club in 1981 there were ten tennis courts, a real pro shop, and over 125 family tennis memberships. The development of the facility and the growth of the membership were quite an accomplishment, but it was the lasting atmosphere of warmth and friendship that helped shape the lives of so many.

It has been 20 years since Pat left East Bay Country Club. The tennis portion of the club closed less than five years after he departed, and still the effect those years had on our lives and the lives of so many of the tennis members is immeasurable! Many of us, still very close friends, talk about the weekends spent, not just on the courts, but barbecuing, visiting, and laughing together.

We made an incredible decision in 1974 to leave our home and our security with three small children; a decision that changed the direction of our lives. It was a gutsy move for us back then, but our spirit of love and our faith and confidence in each other motivated us to take on an exciting adventure.

Fast forward to today: Pat has been a financial planner for the past 20 years. Many of his loyal clients originate from the courts of East Bay where we began our Florida adventure 26 years ago. I am no longer a stay-at-home mom. With our boys all raised and on their own I started my own speaking and training business with Pat's support.

I believe the successes Pat and I have achieved in business, with our three sons, Pat, Jr., David, and Brian, our two daughters-in-law, Kara and Fran, and our many lasting relationships with our friends has so much to do with our liking and believing in each other.

Pat and I are best friends. We were best friends from the beginning and still are. We enjoy each other's company and there is truly no one else with whom we would rather spend time.  There is no one else with whom we feel more comfortable sharing thoughts, feelings, joys, and fears.

## 🍀 Marvin and Vicki Feldman

Marv and Vicki have had a special relationship from the very beginning.  And, I do mean the very beginning!  Their beginning started in second grade in East Liverpool, Ohio. That is when they met and became friends.  They did, however, wait to start dating.  Their first romantic connection was when they were 16 years old at the Key Club Sweetheart Dance.  The next came soon after at the ice-skating pond. From that time forward they have been a truly committed couple.  They are one couple who can honestly say they hardly remember life without each other!

When it came time for college, Marv was given the opportunity to go to any school in the United States he chose and that would accept him.  Vicki was given only one option—a state school.  Since Ohio State was the only choice for Vicki, it became the only choice for Marvin. Having gone all through elementary school and high school together they were determined to attend college together.

They were also determined to get married and they wanted to do it as soon as possible.  In order to do so, one of them had to be out of college.  At the time, Vicki was a pharmacy major in a five-year program.  Her parents (especially her dad) wanted her to pursue a professional career.  Therefore, Marv made it his business to finish his four-year degree in three-and-a-half years.

Marv graduated on March 16th, 1967, they married on March 18th, and Marv started with New York Life Insurance Company on March 27th.

When they married they knew they had to take over all financial responsibilities. This meant Vicki's education became theirs to finance. Vicki had always hated pharmacy so Marv gave her the option, not of quitting college, but changing majors. She transferred into early childhood education.

Before they married both Marv and Vicki's parents always worried that Vicki would get pregnant. After they married, their parents worried Vicki would never get pregnant. When they announced they were expecting their first child after five years of marriage Marv's Mom exclaimed, "We thought you didn't know how!"

One of the things Marv likes most about Vicki is that she is such a caring person. She is always looking to take care of him and the family. She is always "doing" for Marv and the family. Actually, the truth is, they are always "thinking" and "doing" for each other. I will expand on this in the chapter on "Kisses, Hugs, and More."

One of the things Vicki admires most about Marv is his integrity both in business and in personal relationships. His integrity was evident from the beginning of their marriage when they chose to stay in Columbus, Ohio for two main reasons. First, Marv wanted Vicki to have the opportunity to complete her education at Ohio State. Second, Marv wanted to establish himself in the life insurance business independent of his father. At the time, Marv's father, Ben Feldman, was the top producing life insurance agent in the world! Ben had built his business as a New York Life agent in the small town of East Liverpool, Ohio during the years Marv was growing up. Marv could have assured his financial success by going straight into business with his father, but he chose not to.

Vicki totally supported this decision. She had the utmost confidence that Marv could succeed on his own. She had faith in his brains, his abilities and above all, his integrity.

Marv started college as an accounting major, but after one boring quarter transferred into marketing and economics. In his senior year Marv was interviewed on campus by all the large corporations, IBM, Xerox, General Motors, etc. During the interviews they would always ask how much he expected to earn and how soon. After he gave his answer they each had the same reaction—laughter! Marv realized, then, that his financial bar was set a lot higher than the large corporations were willing to go. Thus, he entered the field of insurance.

He became a New York Life agent, not with his father in East Liverpool, but in Columbus, Ohio. He consciously chose to separate himself from his father to prove he could make it on his own. Still the other agents would give his father credit for his good months, saying Ben must have helped him with the sales. The annoying thing was they were quick to give full credit to Marv alone for the bad months. This prompted him to go into management after just two-and-a-half years as an agent. In management he would be the only one who could get the credit (or the blame) for the training and development of new agents.

Marv and Vicki's liking, loving, and undying support and devotion have carried them to great heights both in business and with their family. Marv will be president of Million Dollar Round Table (MDRT) in 2002. MDRT is the most prestigious international organization in the insurance industry. Their two beautiful daughters, Terri and Barbi, have matured into independent, successful, well-adjusted young ladies. Through all their years of business accomplishments and dedication to their family they have also managed to pursue many exciting and varied activities. I will expand on all of these in the chapter on Unity.

## 🍀 Jerry and Melody Figurski

The liking, respect, and deep admiration Jerry and Melody have for each other has not only nourished their relationship for over thirty-three years, but has also carried them through some extremely challenging times. A couple who did not share their special depth of love and commitment would not have survived the challenges they have had to endure.

Jerry and Melody's first major challenge came following early years of financial struggles and work overload. They decided they were ready to have a baby even though they knew that financially they should wait the two years until Jerry graduated from law school.  Their daughter, Tracy, was born both mentally and physically challenged.

Another formidable challenge occurred nine years ago when Melody was diagnosed with breast cancer. The amazing thing about them is that their undue share of difficulties only seems to strengthen their relationship. They continue to grow stronger and stronger as individuals, as a couple, and as a family!

Jerry and Melody met at Kent State University in 1963. They were both working on a political campaign for a mutual friend.  Jerry, taken immediately by Melody's outgoing, fun loving nature, was interested in pursuing a romantic relationship.  However, Melody was not at a stage in her life where she was ready for any serious commitments.  She was, just then, starting to enjoy college life and the dating scene. Looking back on the situation, Jerry feels that he might have frightened Melody in the beginning by the seriousness of his intentions.

The important thing is they became friends—good friends. Their friendship kept growing and growing, creating a solid foundation for their amazing life of commitment to each other. They sealed their commitment when Melody said, "Yes" and they married in 1967.

Their first years, with few dollars and few hours together, were made even harder after Tracy was born.  Staying at home alone with their child who was diagnosed as brain damaged was very stressful for Melody. Yet she never ever considered asking Jerry to give up his dream of obtaining a law degree. Melody says her love for him, as well as her pride in his intelligence, would not allow her to do that. Jerry proved her right and made her proud by graduating first in his night school law class.

Jerry is quick to share the credit with Melody for his successes both as an individual and as an attorney. He believes Melody's love and respect for him have been critical in both his personal and business growth through the years. For one thing, Jerry was basically a shy young man when they met. Melody, on the other hand, was, and still is, an outgoing individual. She can walk into any room and take it over. She captures everyone's attention with her sense of humor, her jokes, and her wonderful story telling.

Although Jerry would probably not be considered shy today, he says he still feels the need to ease slowly into a room, especially with a group of people he does not know. He attributes overcoming most of his shyness to feeling good about himself and to Melody's continued love and respect. Melody laid the foundation years ago and has continued to validate and encourage Jerry through the years.

Another part of Jerry that Melody admires is his caring and giving nature. He has been busy building his successful law practice, yet he has never lost sight of giving to her, their family, and the community. Today he is still an active community volunteer.

Jerry's community involvement is so extensive it would take pages and pages to record it all.

Some of his most outstanding contributions have been made on the Board of the Foundation for the Upper Pinellas Association for Retarded Citizens. He served as president of the Foundation from 1994-1996. He has also been extremely active with the Bar Associations serving as President as well as chairing their Golf Tournament. The communities of Clearwater and Countryside have also benefitted from Jerry's active involvement on numerous boards. He has received many designations and awards for all his contributions. He was named to Who's Who in Florida, America South and Southwest, American Law, Emerging Leaders in America, and Leading American Attorneys. Among other things this year he was selected "Mr. Countryside."

Melody has been primarily a stay-at-home mom through their years together. She held a few positions to help make ends meet early on, but her major role has been as wife and mother. If she ever considered doing otherwise, their daughter's physical and emotional needs put an end to those thoughts. Melody uses the time she manages to get away from family obligations to volunteer in the community. And, that she has done in a big way.

Jerry describes Melody as an exceptional person who loves with intensity. Giving is her life's code. He says whatever she does, whether at home, raising their two children, or volunteering, she is at full throttle. This is quite evident when looking at her active volunteer membership on numerous community associations and boards.

Since 1978 she has been active with the Junior League of Clearwater-Dunedin where she held many positions including President in 1984. She has also worked with the Upper Pinellas Association for Retarded Citizens (UPARC), where she served on both the Agency and the Foundation Board of Directors, Pinellas County Schools, Countryside Country Club, and the American Cancer Society. She has been an active member of Leadership Pinellas since 1996. Melody has received awards and honors from the Clearwater Kiwanis Club (Marion P. Smith Award, 1999), the Clearwater East and Countryside Rotary Clubs (Mrs. Countryside, 1997), Countryside Country Club (Magnificent Member Award, 1997), Delta Gamma (The Oxford Award received by only eight alumni nationally in 1995), and the Tampa Bay Buccaneers (Ultimate Fan Award in 2000 in the Football Hall of Fame in Canton, Ohio).

Even when Melody was undergoing chemotherapy she maintained her upbeat personality and amazing sense of humor. This story demonstrates how her sense of humor kept things in perspective during some rough times. One day while she was walking to her car in the parking lot of the mall someone yelled from across the lot, "I love your hair!" Melody's hair was in the first stages of growing back—still shorter than a crew cut. She looked up to see a woman with the same hairdo. The woman pointed to her own head and said, "Vidal Sassoon, London!" Melody could not resist and replied, "Chemotherapy, Morton Plant Hospital!" The poor woman looked quite flustered as she apologized. Melody thought to herself, "My hairdo was even more expensive than hers!"

Jerry and Melody have experienced challenges that would have destroyed most other couples and, yet, they have not only survived these challenges, but also have maintained their love, commitment, and appreciation for life in the process. Their daughter, Tracy, now lives in a UPARC group home that she moved into in 1993. Tracy has a wonderful, upbeat attitude and personality. Their son, David, born November 30th, 1975 received an engineering degree from the University of Florida, married in 2000 and is now in graduate school at the University of Texas with his wife. Jerry and Melody beam with pride when they speak of their children.

Jerry and Melody have been through many difficult times and yet they still remain best friends. Their liking and loving each other has not only helped them survive challenges and hardships others could not endure, but it has helped them maintain a very "lucky" marriage.

### 🍀 Joe and Harriet Coren

Joe and Harriet Coren have liked and loved each other for more than 53 years! Harriet admires Joe's easygoing nature. She likes that Joe appears to be worry-free most of the time. She often jokes that Joe does not have to worry because she worries enough for both of them. Joe freely admits that Harriet makes most of the decisions in their lives. This arrangement works for them. Joe lets Harriet take charge of every day decisions, saving his input for the more important major life choices.

When it comes to the large decisions, Joe is a very big part of the decision making process. For instance, in 1965 Joe thought long and hard, planning carefully for the purchase of a small run-down luncheonette in Drexel Hill, PA. They sold their suburban home, drained their children's college savings fund, and emptied the family checkbook to fix up "The Trolley Stop."

For three long years they worked seven days a week from sunup to way past sundown to build up their business. Joe loved it. He whistled while he worked. Harriet hated it. She complained while she worked. She never stopped complaining or working until the day that they sold it. The key is they worked it together. They made enough of a profit to move them to Florida, which Harriet is the first to concede now, was more than worth it.

Joe admires Harriet's willingness to take charge, to take care of their everyday needs in a confident manner. Harriet respects Joe's intuition and his ability to use his calm, thoughtful reasoning to deal with some of the larger challenges they have had to manage over the last 53 years.

## ♥ John Green and Susan Capio

John and Susan have known each other for over 19 years. Since meeting in 1982 their lives together have taken many exciting, diverse, and challenging directions.

What John loved about Susan in the beginning was her confident, optimistic outlook. He believed this confidence and optimism coupled with her intelligence and "people smart" skills would take Susan to the top of the medical industry. And, it did!

After a short stint teaching, Susan became a sales representative for a medical company in 1984. Six years later Susan was promoted to sales manager in Tampa, Florida. She was one of only four female managers out of the hundred national managers to hold that position. Her sales area did so well that just four years later she was promoted once again this time to regional sales manager in New York. She was the only female in that position. Her region did extremely well going to number one nationally. It held the number one spot until Susan was promoted in July 2000 to president of the entire southeastern region. The only female ever to hold the position of president!

Yes, John loved Susan because she was smart, optimistic, confident, fun, and loving. It is these qualities John admired so much that brought Susan to great heights in her business career.

It was John's kind, stable, and loving nature that attracted Susan. Susan thrived on being on the go and on the rise. She loved the fact that John was not only stable, but also smart. John was supposed to keep them in balance and their lives on a more grounded course.

Susan's continuous promotions necessitated moves from Florida to New York and then, just seven years later, from New York back down to Florida. These were not easy moves. Add to it the fact that Susan was pregnant with their oldest daughter during the first big move to New York. During their move back to Florida their daughters were only six and three. They had to adjust to a new environment, new friends, and a new school. John, unfortunately, was still employed in New York at the time Susan and the girls made the move to Central Florida. They thought bringing their nanny with them to Florida would aid in the transition.

There was a great need for John and Susan to work together during these times of change and challenge. Strong communication, unity of interests, unity of spirit, and a clear understanding of their individual needs, their daughters' needs and the family needs were required. Unfortunately, their relationship was not strong enough to make these very difficult transitions go smoothly. The days of change and challenge became frustrating and unsettling—especially for John.

❀❀❀

Liking each other is a most important ingredient in a "L.U.C.K.Y." MARRIAGE. Here are some basics for the "L" in a "L.U.C.K.Y." marriage:

## CHECKLIST FOR THE "L"

__1.   LIKE THE BASIC CHARACTER OF YOUR SPOUSE.

__2.   LIKE HOW YOUR SPOUSE TREATS FAMILY AND FRIENDS.

__3.   LIKE THE PERSONALITY OF YOUR SPOUSE.

__4.   PICK A FRIEND FOR LIFE.

__5.   DO NOT PLAN ON CHANGING YOUR SPOUSE.

__6.   WHAT YOU SEE IS WHAT YOU GET!

__7.   LOVE WITHOUT LIKE TURNS INTO DISLIKE.

__8.   LIKE WITHOUT LOVE CAN GROW INTO LOVE!

# CHAPTER TWO

## "U"

### "U" Stands for Unity

Unity is so encompassing. There are so many areas in which it can and should exist in a marriage. Some areas include unity of spirit, family, (couple, children, extended family), activities, interests, living environment, religion, goals, nationality, traditions, education, and commitment. No marriage will share all the areas of unity. Some will have many more areas than others. Some marriages can be "lucky" even though certain areas do not exist. One example I can think of is unity of religion. There are some very strong marriages in which spouses are of different religions. In fact some of the "lucky" couples represented in this book have different religious backgrounds. This will be discussed at length later in the chapter. There are a few areas of unity I think are necessary for "lucky" marriages to exist.

23

## UNITY OF SPIRIT

A couple needs to have unity of spirit, heart, and commitment—commitment to the institution of marriage—commitment to each other. After you select the person you are going to marry, then you must make this commitment a priority. Plan on a lifetime commitment with the person you have chosen to like, love, and care for the rest of your life. It is this devotion to each other that will create one spirit.

*❀❀❀ Commitment to marriage and*
*each other is essential ❀❀❀*

Commitment appears to be easy at the time you say, "I do." But, for some it becomes a life-long challenge or a not so long challenge, which ends in divorce. Life takes many turns, many different directions. It is only through unity of spirit and commitment that a couple can take all the turns and directions together as a team. It is true especially in this modern world of two-career families.

Back in the 60's when couples married, the first year or so was a time for adjustment, a time to adjust to their new living arrangements. (Most couples did not live together before marriage back then.) It was a time to work, save, and plan for their future together. After the first few years most marriages fell into rather a set routine. In today's world there are continuing adjustments and decisions: where to live, what schooling should take priority, what career direction is most important, and for which spouse. There are so many more adjustments that were not as prevalent in previous generations. Challenges arise from the very beginning and continue throughout the relationship.

John Green and Susan Capio are perfect examples of the modern day two-career families. Their lives have taken so many changes of direction due to education and career moves. The geographic re-locations prompted by Susan's promotions have required many critical adjustments for John and Susan as individuals, as a couple, and as a family. These adjustments are now taking a toll on their relationship.

*❀❀❀ Adjustments are a constant part*
*of any marriage ❀❀❀*

Even with all these added choices the one choice, the one decision that should not be adjusted or ignored is the priority of the relationship—the couple.

Throughout a lifetime I can not conceive of the success of the marriage unless this total commitment to the oneness and spirit of the marriage is a priority. There are too many pressures and outside forces to have a "lucky" marriage without total commitment.

## FAMILY UNITY

Family is the most crucial point of unity.  Within the family issue come some very important and very critical issues.

The first, of course, is selecting your mate.  Once chosen, your spouse becomes your primary family unit.  You two are the center of your family and your future family.  The second decision, a decision I believe should be made before marriage, is whether you will or will not have children.

*❁❁❁ Select a mate for life ❁❁❁*

The choice to have or not to have children is probably the most life-altering decision a couple will ever make.  Although I very much believe in the commitment of marriage, I also believe wrong choices are sometimes made.  Wrong choices can and should be reconsidered and possibly dissolved before children are brought into the relationship.  Once children are involved, the ending of the relationship is no longer a viable option.  Yes, you can still get a divorce; however, children create ties and involvement that last for life.

After children are brought into the family, I believe every possible effort should be made to keep a marriage together.

*❁❁❁ The decision to have or not to have children*
*is one that should be made*
*before the decision to marry ❁❁❁*

Things have changed in this modern generation. Through the 1960's, when you got married, you were expected to stay married. Since the 60's the divorce rate has been on a steady rise. Marriage has been affected a lot by the "me" times we live in. If I am not happy in a place, a job, or a relationship, I will just simply end it and move on. This attitude, of going into a marriage with the idea that you can leave at any time if you do not like it, is sure to cause more divorces.

I think there needs to be a middle of the road here. Some marriages should never be and perhaps need to be dissolved, but others need to be worked on and saved especially after the addition of children.

❀❀❀ *Children bind you forever* ❀❀❀

Some couples try to make adjustments when they begin to realize that their marriage is not what they expected it to be. Unfortunately, some of these couples think that having children will mend their failing marriages. Children will not strengthen a weak marriage! It does not work that way. Children will not improve an unhappy marriage, in fact, they are sure to add to the challenges. Children should be added to the family unit only when a couple feels comfortable and secure in their own relationship.

❀❀❀ *Do not have children*
*to try to help your marriage* ❀❀❀

Select your mate carefully.  Select a person with whom you desire to spend the rest of your life.  It is a most important decision.  Take the time to get to know this person. Take the time to share your thoughts, your interests, your dreams, and your goals. Take the time to discuss the major issue of children.  Do you want children or do you want to focus on other things?  Things may change after you are married; there are no guaranties, but be as prepared as possible.

## COUPLE UNITY

The unity of the couple establishes the strength of the entire family. The togetherness and oneness of the couple is the key to a healthy family. It is not possible to have a fully successful family relationship without this powerful unit of oneness. Some families do survive and are fairly successful in meeting the needs of their children without this special unity of heart and spirit, but there is a much greater level of success if oneness of spirit is attained and maintained!

How do couples establish and maintain a oneness of heart and spirit? It is not always easy, but it can and should be done to maintain a "lucky" marriage.

MAKE YOUR RELATIONSHIP A PRIORITY. This is so important it bears repeating and repeating! MAKE YOUR RELATIONSHIP A PRIORITY.

From the moment you take your vows you should never lose sight of this priority. School, business, work, prior commitments, special interests, and children can take up your time and interfere with your continuing relationship. There is nothing you are doing, no other commitments as important as your relationship with your spouse.

Make time! Set a schedule that includes "lone" time with your spouse. In this modern world couples get so tied up in "doing" and "being" they sometimes lose sight of their most important responsibility: the responsibility of keeping their relationship alive.

29

### ❀❀❀ *Make Your Relationship a Priority* ❀❀❀

Children are an added challenge to a couple's relationship. They can be a very fulfilling and loving addition to the couple's lives. They can also be a huge distraction to the couple's primary relationship. Talk about commitment of time, energy, and focus! Children can be all that and more. Children often become the center of family life. It is wonderful to devote energy and commitment to children, but not at the expense of the couple. The couple must still maintain their separate relationship.

### ❀❀❀ *Always remember to set time to be a couple* ❀❀❀

How often have you heard of couples who have devoted their whole lives to their children, only to find out that when their children leave home they no longer have anything in common? The children became their one common interest. The children kept them distracted from their relationship for 20 to 25 years! Now there are no children and no relationship!

Make an effort to keep the relationship alive! This may take a specific plan—scheduling of time. Schedule times together each day, each week, and/or each month. It can be as simple as a meal out or an evening stroll—perhaps a weekend retreat without the children. We all have different amounts of time available in our lives, but the point is whatever time there is available should be dedicated to a most important relationship—the couple!

*The couple is the primary family unit*

## 🍀 Pat and Judy Siracusa

Pat and I bonded so quickly and so naturally. From the very beginning of our relationship we seemed to be of one spirit. The concept of togetherness, oneness, and unity of commitment was never a problem for us as a couple. That is not to say we did not experience adjustments along the way. Extended family was our biggest challenge in the early days of our marriage. However, before I get into those issues, let me first talk about us as a couple.

In the three years before our first son was born we enjoyed our life as a couple, spending all of our free time together in the activities we both love. Our relationship needed an adjustment after the birth of Pat, Jr. Our very full lives became even fuller. The time we had spent alone together had been eliminated by the presence of our new baby. It was a situation that actually hit us by surprise. We had not seriously thought about the total time commitment of the baby. We knew it was a major, full-time job, but realistically we did not understand that our time alone would be all but eliminated.

Pat was still teaching, coaching, and playing in some sports leagues at the time. I, however, suddenly became a stay-at-home mom beginning to miss, and probably resent, the lack of outside activities. I felt guilty complaining about not getting out. I tried not to. I thought the baby was my responsibility. Yet one night when Pat came home from his touch football league, I had had it. I was dressed and ready to go out. Pat said, "What are you doing?" "I just need to get out," was all I could say. "Well, where are you going?" "Just out. Pat, Jr. is in bed. Please stay home with him so I can get out of here!" "O.K. but I don't understand. Where are you going?" he asked again. "I'm not sure. Shopping, I guess." Even with my frustration coming out at that very moment I still could not verbalize what I was feeling. Pat ran next door, asked our neighbor to baby-sit, and came out with me that night. That was all it took. After that evening we sat down and discussed our schedules, our needs, and our time together, or our lack of time together. We set a plan for "us."

Since that night, I do not think Pat and I have ever gone a week without spending quality time together. We spent a lot of time with our children through the years. We attended practically every activity in which they were involved, but not at the expense of our time together. When the children were young we made Friday night "our night." We would have a quiet fondue dinner and a peaceful evening together. As the children got older we changed "our time" to Friday afternoons. Whether it was a walk on the beach, lunch, or hitting tennis balls together; it was "our time." To this day our boys still ask, "It's Friday afternoon, what are you two going to do today?"

Pat and I have so many interests we share that we never were at a loss to find activities to do together. The challenge was finding the time. Because we did make a conscious effort to make the time during the stages when time was very limited, today as "empty nesters" we are still enjoying each other and our time together.

## 🍀 Marvin and Vicki Feldman

Marv and Vicki always knew they wanted children. Of this there was never any doubt. They are people who plan and prepare. They felt there was time. They wanted to use the time available to get to know each other even better. They also wanted to enjoy their freedom, build their business, and enjoy their hobbies. When they married Vicki still had a few more years of school to complete and then she wanted to teach. During this "child-free" period they were heavily involved in race cars. They purchased a corvette that they both raced competitively against the clock.

Five years and one dog later they were ready to have their first child. Having practiced their parenting skills on their Dalmatian, it is hard to believe they ever felt ready to parent a child. From what I heard about the training successes, or lack thereof with their dog, it is amazing they decided to have children at all. They said their dog was never intelligent enough to be trained, but thankfully their children were!

After their first daughter, Terri, was born they found they could still continue to do the things they loved to do. They even managed to continue racing. They would bundle Terri up and take her to the track with them. They took turns. One held the baby and the other would race. Sometimes Vicki's parents, who were three-and-a-half-hours away, would come and stay with Terri while they took off for a weekend of racing. One weekend at Indianapolis they blew their engine and ended up just simply spending the whole weekend alone together. Nine months later Barbi was born! This is when things really changed. Marv and Vicki could maneuver one child, but two, just 18 months apart, made the maneuvering too challenging.

Time for hobbies became very limited after their second daughter was born. Adjustments had to be made. They sold their 1970 Corvette to purchase living room furniture. Having lost their competitive edge on the track they found other things to do with the time they had available for themselves.

They made Saturday night their night. It might be a movie, the theater, or even just locking themselves in their bedroom. Saturday and Sunday were always family time. Marv and Vicki both spent a lot of time involved in their daughters' activities, but they never let a week pass without their "couple time" or as Marv and Vicki referred to it, "off duty mom and dad" time.

The Feldmans were also very fortunate that Vicki's parents allowed them the opportunity to do some business travel without worrying about the girls. Vicki's mom and dad would move in and take over. The girls never missed activities; never had to adjust schedules. Marv and Vicki would sometimes have to be gone for two or three weeks at a time, but the girls never felt abandoned because "Pop

Pop" and "Nanna" loved them and cared for them just like mom and dad.

The Feldmans have dedicated themselves to their business and their family through the years. But, with equal devotion and commitment, they have dedicated themselves to each other. It is this devotion to each other that has contributed to their successes both in business and with their family.

## 🍀 Jerry and Melody Figurski

A couple is challenged when children are brought into the family unit. This was compounded for Jerry and Melody since their first child was physically and mentally disabled. Couple time was difficult to find after Tracy was born, but find it they did!

Jerry and Melody have always cherished their shared time together so they have always made a conscious effort to get as much of that time as possible. They created time even in those first few years when Jerry was working and going to law school. They set up priorities for their life and their very limited budget: rent, food, and then a caregiver—whenever possible.

After Jerry's graduation from law school and their move to Florida, help from grandparents was not possible. Jerry's parents were 1100 miles away and Melody's parents both worked. At that point, however, their financial situation improved greatly, allowing them more freedom to hire caregivers. Unfortunately, finding willing, as well as ac-

35

ceptable, caregivers for a special needs child increased the challenge. Once their son, David, turned 11 or 12 he became their answer to an evening out alone. David was wonderful with Tracy. They paid him to care for her, as they would any other "sitter," but never asked him to give up his own activities to sit for Tracy.

Jerry and Melody love spending time together. Couple time is so precious to them. Therefore, it has been and always will be a priority.

## 🍀 Joe and Harriet Coren

Each couple has different needs. Joe and Harriet did not take a lot of time to do activities as a couple when their children were growing up. They spent a great deal of time together but it was time spent around the house.

When their children were just one and three years old, Harriet was hospitalized for ten days. Joe needed to hire a housekeeper to help him with their home and the children. After Harriet came home from the hospital Joe kept the housekeeper for an extra two days so he and Harriet could get away together to visit friends—a rarity for the Corens!

The only activity they pursued without their children was bowling. They bowled in a couples' league one evening a week for a number of years. Joe and Harriet made it through the child rearing years without lots of couple activities. Each couple is different. They maintained a "lucky" marriage without a lot of couple time. This is rare and would not work for most couples. It worked for them. I would not recommend this for most couples.

##  John Green and Susan Capio

John Green and Susan Capio are now in the middle of the most critical time for maintaining couple unity. Business commitments and the demands of their young daughters are both at their highest levels. It is challenging for them to find time to do everything. Unfortunately, sometimes we get caught doing what appears to be "the necessities," letting go of things that do not appear as critical. John and Susan believe business and the girls are most critical. The thing getting eliminated is "couple time." My belief is "couple time" is critical and the lack of it is beginning to take a huge effect on their lives!

John and Susan dated five years before marrying. They then spent seven years as DINKS (Dual Income No Kids). During these years they spent a lot of time together traveling, building a home, and prospering financially. In the twelve years before they had children they believed they had the opportunity to get to know and bond with each other. By the time the girls came along they felt "mentally ready." They say they do not feel cheated by their limited time together. "Been there, done that!"

It is hard for them to juggle everything. I understand this. But, it is my strong opinion that John and Susan need to add more couple time into their "juggling act." Now they feel the girls must be their priority, however, the girls will be around for a long time. When the time comes for their daughters to move on, will "dad" and "mom" be around to become John and Susan again?  "Couple time" is critical!

❀❀❀

Unity of the couple must be kept as a priority.  It is the unity of the couple and the closeness of the relationship that keeps the changing directions, difficult decisions, and challenges all in perspective.  Making time together keeps the oneness and spirit alive.  It also has an effect on your communication and your common interests.  Difficult choices—major life choices are more easily made and kept in perspective when two people are making and supporting them together.

*❀❀❀ Together, as one unit,*
*change your directions,*
*make major decisions and life choices ❀❀❀*

## EXTENDED FAMILY

At the time you marry, your parents, brothers, and sisters, change from being your primary family to your extended family. This can be a major adjustment for some newly-weds who have trouble letting go of their original, established support system and focus of family life. And, it can be an even greater challenge to some parents who have trouble sharing their child. Some parents simply have difficulty letting go of control. Some parents may view the new spouse more as an intruder than a new family member. Differences in religion, nationalities, traditions, etc., can add to even greater adjustments. The challenge to include and unite as new members enter a family can be a large one.

*When you marry*
*your spouse becomes*
*your primary family*

Each family has different concepts of "family." Some believe family means blood relatives. In-laws, therefore, are not considered true family. They are viewed as people who must be included in the family, but are not really family. They are individuals with whom the true family, the blood relatives, must learn to contend. Neither the parents, nor brothers and sisters get to choose whom their children or siblings marry. They may express their doubts, they may not approve, and they may sincerely dislike the chosen spouse, but they are not the ones who make the final choice.

It can become a large challenge, both for the family who has difficulty accepting "the outsider" and for the new "relative" who must try to be accepted.  But it is a challenge that must be dealt with and resolved in order to maintain a "lucky" marriage.  The extended family (your spouse's parents, spouse's siblings, and other relatives such as aunts, uncles, cousins, etc.) is an important part of the whole relationship.

Hopefully, it is a comfortable transition.  Sometimes it is. In some cases both the new spouse and the newly acquired family genuinely like each other and bond quite naturally.  They may have known each other for a long time or they may just meet and take an immediate liking to each other.  This is great!  For some, unfortunately, it is not that easy.  There may be resistance on the part of either the spouse's family or the new spouse or both.

Let's look at ways to develop a relationship between the extended family and the new spouse.  First, keep in mind that most relationships take time. Allow time to get to know and feel comfortable with each other.  Do not push your way into a relationship, especially if the other person or persons seem reluctant to accept it.  Establish grounds of mutual interests, understanding, and agreement.  It is just like developing any other relationship.  It takes time, common interests, and mutual respect.  As it is important to build and maintain your couple relationship, it is also important a to try to build and maintain your extended family relationships.

*Take time to build a relationship*
*with extended family*

One major barrier with the in-law relationship as opposed to the couple relationship is that the in-laws did not necessarily choose each other and may not be as anxious for it to work.

If the in-law relationship is difficult at first, it is important to keep in mind that there is much to be gained from building a good relationship; and lots more to be lost by not developing the relationship. In-laws have many mutual interests and many more common bonds that can and will develop during future years if given the opportunity.

The relationship can be made stronger by making a conscious effort to spend quality time together, finding interests in common, and learning to communicate as often and as effectively as possible with each other.

*♧♧♧ Take time to develop communication, interests, and common bonds with your spouse's family ♧♧♧*

## ♣ Pat and Judy Siracusa

When Pat and I married we made a conscious decision to move to a neutral location away from both sets of parents. The decision was not based on a lack of family love or belief in family ties. It was based upon our need to have time and space to focus on building our own union together. We believed in the importance of family then, as we do today. However, we knew it would be necessary to first establish ourselves as a couple outside of family influence.

As I stated before, each family has a different concept of "family." Growing up, I never knew much difference between blood relatives and in-laws. My parents' families grew up next door to each other and were all friends. There was never any distinction between who was related to whom. We were all one family. In Pat's family it was a different situation. There was his father's family and his mother's family—two very separate units. Pat's folks, therefore, were brought up in an environment in which family was family; in-laws were in-laws.

When I met his folks they viewed me, I believe, as a potential daughter-in-law. Although I was like them in that I was both Italian and Catholic, I was not from Buffalo. I was from Westchester, New York. I am sure it was a difficult time for them. In turn, they made it a very difficult time for Pat and me.

My in-laws, who were naturally very warm and social people, treated me with reserve and control. Being a very warm and social person myself, I believed it would be just a matter of time before things would change. Unfortunately, it was not that easy.

Pat and I dated for four years before we married. Because we were in college at a location half way between both of our hometowns, we were only able to spend a limited amount of time with each other's families. I did not get to establish a comfortable rapport with his parents.

In 1965 when we scheduled our wedding Pat's parents threatened not to attend. Looking back on it, they probably reacted this way because in their minds they were losing their son. This, of course, was still extremely upsetting for us.

In the first years of our marriage we made an effort to spend vacations and holidays with Pat's family. They were an eight-hour car ride away and it was the only time we had to see them. My parents were less than two hours away so we could visit with them on weekends. Through the years Pat's parents and I maintained our polite, reserved relationship.

Our decision to move even further away after nine years of marriage was probably not a very popular decision with either set of parents. We made the decision based on our immediate family needs and desires, not on the needs and desires of extended family.

We saw the move as an opportunity for Pat to develop a tennis business and for us to enjoy a home under sunny skies and warm weather. In many ways it was one of the best decisions of our lives. Unfortunately it did limit the natural development of extended family relations.

Because we did not have extended family around us, our friends became our extended family. Holidays and special occasions were shared with them. We developed a warm, loving network of friends. Our business careers and our three sons all flourished. In retrospect, the downside of our move was the unfortunate lack of extended family participation in our lives and the lives of our boys. I reiterate "time together," "interests in common," and "time to communicate" are all needed to develop and maintain strong relationships. The distance, and the lack of time together, did not allow for the natural growth of extended family ties.

Extended family time was very limited after our move to Florida. Due to our lack of time and our lack of funds, Pat and I and the boys were not able to make many trips up north, naturally distancing us even more. Visits from our parents were also limited.

My parents, who lived in New Jersey at the time, would make two trips each year, staying with us a week each time. Pat's folks would make one trip each year, staying in our home for three weeks. Unfortunately, the grandparents did not have time to really get to know their grandsons nor did our boys get to know their grandparents.

Both Pat's parents and my parents had other grandchildren near them in the north and, of course, they developed much closer relationships with them. It is difficult to rush quality time!

For me there was the added challenge of being the hostess during the visits. I wanted everything to go smoothly. I wanted the children to behave and for everyone to get along in the limited time we had together. These times were always exhausting for me.

It was particularly exhausting when Pat's folks came for their three-week stay in our home. All the cooking, cleaning, and caring for the children left me little time to enjoy them, let alone help me develop a closer relationship with them.

It takes a long time to build relationships. Family unity is very much worth the time, patience, and effort. If the effort had not been made we could have destroyed family unity forever. It did take a lot longer than I anticipated, but today, I believe, we have a good relationship.

Pat's father died in a car accident in 1991. About three years ago we helped buy Pat's mom a condo in Clearwater, less than two miles from our home. She is staying in Florida for longer periods of time each year. Mom is a very young, very active "70-something" woman. She has made friends and is involved in many activities at her condo. She has also had the opportunity to get to know and bond with her grandsons and their wives in the last few years. She appears to be very comfortable in our home now.

Think if the effort was not made. Family unity is special and extended family is a very important part of this unity.

Our two older sons are married. Pat, Jr., is a prosecutor in Pinellas County and is married to Kara, a marketing director of an internet company. David is a financial advisor for AXA in Tampa and is married to Fran, a high school Spanish teacher. Our youngest son, Brian, recently moved to San Diego to pursue a career in sports communication. Pat, Jr. and David and their wives have chosen to remain in the area where they grew up and where we still live. We are, of course, pleased to have them around. We hope never to over-impose ourselves in their lives.

45

We all make an effort to get together once a week or so. Most Sundays we have dinner at our home so we can catch up on what the others are doing. We often follow dinner with family tennis, bowling, or another interactive activity. There is no requirement for attendance. Whoever is available and interested gets together, which is most of us, most of the time.

## 🍀 Marvin and Vicki Feldman

Extended family has always been an important part of Marv and Vicki's lives. Their parents each had strong marriages and were great role models. Both their families lived in the small town of East Liverpool, Ohio where they grew up. East Liverpool is the town where Marv and Vicki have lived with their own family most of their lives. It was only for the first seven years of their marriage that they elected to stay in Columbus, Ohio about three-and-a-half-hours away.

Although extended family is an important part of their lives, there were some major issues that had to be resolved at the beginning of their relationship.

Vicki's family was concerned that if Marv and Vicki married too soon, Vicki would not finish college. It was very important to them that she fulfill her potential and graduate from college with a professional degree. After Marv and Vicki got married Vicki's parents said her education would not be their responsibility anymore.

On Marv's side of the family there was strong resistance to accepting Vicki at the beginning. Marvin's family was Jewish. Vicki was not. Marv's mom, who was a very kind, loving person, had real concerns about her son and his future. She truly believed it was important for him to marry a Jewish girl. She kept trying to set him up with a nice Jewish girl! To keep his mom happy Marv went on a few unbelievable dates. Dates that only further convinced him that Vicki Smith was definitely the one for him!

When Marv and Vicki got engaged, Marv's mom conceded. She realized Marvin had made up his mind. Vicki was his choice. Basically, she decided she would rather gain a daughter than lose a son. She became more accepting of Vicki. The fact that Vicki converted to Judaism, I am sure, was also a great comfort to Marv's mom.

In some ways the religious differences actually ended up helping in the area of extended family. There was never any conflict over where to spend religious holidays. Jewish holidays were shared with the Feldmans and Christian holidays with the Smiths.

Marv's mom died a few years after they were married. Unfortunately, she did not have the opportunity to share in their lives or get to know her granddaughters. She would have loved them! Vicki's parents were the kind of grandparents who were always available and willing to be involved in the lives of their grandchildren.

Due to Marv and Vicki's extensive business obligations they often called upon Vicki's parents to take care of the girls.

The wonderful part was that "Pop Pop" and "Nanna" would move into their home and take over the "parenting routine." The girls' lives did not skip a beat. There was no state of upheaval when dad and mom had to take off. After Vicki's dad died in 1986, "Nanna" continued to be their loving caretaker. Both Terri and Barbi are still incredibly close to their grandmother.

Extended family has had a wonderfully positive influence on the lives of the Feldmans. Unfortunately, Marv's parents have both passed on. His father, who died in 1993, had a huge effect on Marv's business career. His dad's success in insurance with New York Life helped influence Marv's decision to go into the field.

When Marv's mom died in 1974, his dad asked Marv to return to East Liverpool and become an agent in the family business. This brought Marv and Vicki and the girls back to the hometown of their families. They have made their home there ever since.

They also own a home in the Tampa Bay area of Florida. Their daughters both attended the University of Florida. After graduation from the University of Florida Law School, Terri moved out to California to pursue a career in the film industry and is still there. She will be returning to Florida to get married this year, but plans on residing in California. After graduating from the University of Florida, Barbi went to Law School in the state of Washington. She returned to Florida, married a fellow attorney, and is planning to remain in Florida. In fact, Barbi hopes to move from the east coast of Florida to the west coast to be even closer to her parents.

Marv and Vicki are very close with the girls. Though they may not be able to see them as often as they would like, they are in constant communication with them.

### ☘ Jerry and Melody Figurski

Extended family was one of the first big hurdles for Jerry and Melody. Melody's family was not a problem. Melody's dad had experienced the challenges of dealing with differences in a marriage. His father was a minister and he had married a Roman Catholic. The major concern of Melody's dad was that Melody loved Jerry. Once he established that Melody really loved Jerry, both of Melody's parents accepted him warmly. Ever since, Melody's family has been a very important part of their lives. They are among their best friends. They enjoy spending time "going and doing" or just being at home with them having a good family discussion.

With Jerry's family it was different. Melody was definitely not what Jerry's parents had planned for their son. She was not Polish, she was not from their hometown and, most importantly, she was not Catholic! Jerry's family lived their entire lives in a town of 900 people and about 890 were Polish Catholics. This is what they knew. Looking back, it is easy now for Melody to understand how hard it was for them! Melody can remember Jerry's mom saying, "Melody, it is nothing personal, dear. We wouldn't like you if you were Queen Elizabeth."

However, they soon realized Jerry had made up his mind and there was no changing it. On their wedding day the Figurski's gave them their complete blessing. Although they made an effort to accept Melody, it took Melody time to get over the uncomfortable feeling of knowing she was from a different background and certainly not what they had planned on. The main focus in life for Jerry's mother has always been her family. She is a true matriarch. Therefore, it was very difficult for her to give up control of her son to another woman. It was comforting, on some level, for Melody to be told by one of her sisters-in-law that it had been the same with each of her daughters-in-law. Mom Figurski just did not like having her sons "stolen" away from her. She does, however, have a large capacity to love (similar to her daughter-in-law, Melody) so getting to know and like Melody made the relationship much, much better. Today, Mom Figurski and Melody are very close!

Melody says when her son, David, married it made her much more understanding of her mother-in-law's feelings. David married a wonderful girl, Melissa, whom Melody loves. And, still it is an adjustment to lose him in many ways to another woman. She can only imagine the emotions of a mother who "loses" her son to a woman with such a different background.

Jerry and Melody moved from Ohio to Florida in large part to be near Melody's parents. Melody missed having them as a part of their lives and the lives of their children. It was a very difficult decision because this meant having to move farther away from Jerry's family. Although Melody let Jerry make the final decision she has always felt some guilt about the move. She knows it was hard on Jerry then and, in some ways, still is. The move definitely drew him away from his extended family.

## 🍀 Joe and Harriet Coren

Joe and Harriet now have children and grandchildren spread from Philadelphia to North Carolina to Florida.

Their family is still the main focus in their lives so they have set up a system to stay in touch as often as possible. Unfortunately, their visits are limited to a couple of times a year, but they never let a week go by without speaking on the phone. Emails, with the unique ability to include pictures and videos, have also increased their communication.

## 💔 John Green and Susan Capio

John and Susan say they have tried to keep a balance with extended families. One way they have done so is by dividing the holidays between the two families. They chose to keep their respective extended families from influencing such major decisions as location moves, promotions, and religion.

Susan is quite satisfied with the lack of family involvement in their lives. John, on the other hand, was stressed by having to live up north so far away from family for such a long time.  He really missed the participation of family in his life and the lives of their children.

❀❀❀

In today's world, newly married couples often move even greater distances away from their families.  Meeting in college they may come from very distant parts of the world.  Also, with all the varied opportunities in education, jobs, and business ventures young people have the need to move and perhaps keep moving in many different directions.

*❀❀❀ Work to establish good family relationships
for the sake of the whole family unit ❀❀❀*

Families, therefore, must make an even greater effort to keep in touch.  Luckily there are more means of doing so in this modern, high tech world via email, cell phones, and the more economic airfares available.  While it is easier to keep in touch, the key still is to make the effort.

Many of my friends who are now grandparents, make special efforts to have as much quality time with their distant children and grandchildren as possible.  They telephone, email, and travel as frequently as possible.  Baby-sitting for your grandchildren sure helps build strong relationships not only with the grandchildren, but also with the very thankful parents.  All relationships take time, effort, and focus, but the results are more than worth it!

52

## NATIONALITY and RACE

Nationality and race are defining aspects of each spouse's make-up that, of course, cannot be altered. Spouses of different nationality or race will often face added challenges in their marriages. Values, traditions, and lifestyles may all vary. Views on education, finances, holidays, living conditions, and much more can be influenced by diverse backgrounds.

Problems can develop from both within the family and without. Outsiders sometimes take a negative view of mixed marriages. This discrimination can cause added challenges especially for the children.

## UNITY OF INTERESTS

It is so important in a relationship to have interests in common. There are so many different interests a couple can share—playing sports, playing cards, watching sports, dancing, shopping, home decorating, gardening, movies, music, dining, traveling, friends, volunteer work, reading, theater, professions, lovemaking, etc., etc.

If a couple does not have natural interests in common when they marry it is necessary to develop some. It is important before, during, and after children. As mentioned earlier, some couples have children and let them become the only common bond in their relationship. It is a real shock, then, when the children leave and they have no clue about the person with whom they are now sharing the "empty nest."

*❀❀❀ Develop common interests*
*with your spouse ❀❀❀*

Shared interests help to keep the relationship alive. I spoke earlier about couple time—the priority of the couple. It is much easier to spend time together, if you have interests in common. If you have a passion for an activity—boating, skiing, bowling, or whatever, it makes it that much more compelling to take the time to do these things together.

Developing activities to do together is vital to the couple's relationship. It is important to find common interests that can be shared whether it be walks on the beach, drives in the country, or fine dining.

Search for a few activities that interest both parties, not an interest one loves and the other "goes along with" just to keep peace. There are so many things to do in this world there must be at least one activity that interests both partners. Search for it!

All interests do not have to be shared interests. Many happily married couples share many mutual interests and also pursue separate interests. Having activities that you share with a group of your same sex friends adds variety and sometimes a break to the constant togetherness of a couple. Or some individuals enjoy pursuing lone activities such as fishing, jogging, and hunting. These activities may allow them time to reconnect with themselves and/or nature.

We are all different and, therefore, have different requirements for time together, time with friends, and lone time. However, it is important in the mix to make sure some interests and activities are shared with your spouse.

*Enjoy interests and activities with friends*

### Pat and Judy Siracusa

Pat and I have always had many interests in common. Sports are definitely among our strongest common interests. We love watching sports both in person and on television. Even more, however, we enjoy playing sports. Throughout our early years we played volleyball, soccer, tennis, water-skied, camped, and hiked. We did many of these activities together.

Pat also played in men's basketball, baseball, and tennis leagues. I played in ladies' tennis leagues. When Pat participates in his leagues I become an enthusiastic spectator. He loves having me there—supporting and cheering for him and the team.

An activity I have always participated in without Pat is a lady's bridge group. Playing bridge with a group of seven good friends is an activity I have enjoyed. And, it is certainly not because I am a "bridge guru." It is simply a wonderful time of bonding with the "girls," sharing experiences and sometimes simply venting. During the years when my boys were growing up my bridge club was "my moms' support group." There was always someone in the group who had experienced the same challenges with their children that I was going through. Playing bridge and sharing lives has been great.

In recent years Pat and I have taken up additional activities—activities we were unable to pursue when the children were growing up. Priority of time and money kept us from participating in these activities. We took up snow skiing at the rather advanced age of 52 and have now enjoyed a number of ski vacations over the last five years. We love it! We also took up golf two years ago. I cannot honestly say I love golf. It depends on the day, the time, and the hole! We have also begun to bike a lot more. We went on an awesome biking vacation in Vermont this year.

Other activities Pat and I enjoy together are traveling, dining, walking on the beach, dancing, visiting with friends and family, and, on rare occasions, relaxing together in front of the television.

## 🍀 Marvin and Vicki Feldman

Marv and Vicki have always shared a wide variety of interests. They have participated in many adventurous types of activities throughout the years as well as a lot of relaxing, intellectual activities. In the "pre-children era" they were both involved with race cars and pistol shooting. "Post-children" they gave up the cars and the guns . . . for awhile.

Both Vicki and Marv have always loved to read. They enjoy spending time curled up reading together—with their own books, of course. They like to go to the theater and the movies. Some evenings, they just enjoy staying at home watching television. Art is another passion they both share. Buying art is probably the only impulsive thing they do.

After Terri and Barbi were born they decided, in addition to their couple activities, it would be a good idea for them to also pursue some separate activities. Marv joined a men's pistol club giving him the opportunity to bond with the guys as well as compete a couple of times a week. Although he is not as active as he used to be due to travel, etc., he still maintains his connection with the men and the club.

Vicki's involvement in a separate activity became a dream fulfilled—a true passion—flying! Today Vicki is an experienced pilot. She gained her wings over 23 years ago. Although she knew in her heart she would learn to fly someday, Marv gave her "The Wind Beneath Her Wings" in 1977. Marv was doing business with an air charter company and decided it would be good to own an aircraft and lease it back as a tax write off. When Marv and Vicki went to look at the aircraft, Marv inquired if there were people on staff that could teach Vicki to fly. Marv paid the bills. Vicki flew.

That was just the beginning. Vicki's piloting has been a wonderful contribution not only to her own enjoyment, but it has given them many wonderful hours in the sky together. Marv's business ventures required a lot of travel and with Vicki as his pilot they could do it together.

As Vicki crawled out of the cockpit, Marv loved to introduce her to his clients. "I would like you to meet my pilot . . . and my mistress." After an uncomfortable pause he would add, "She is also my wife!"

In the past few years they have traveled together more than ever. As a member of the Executive Committee of Million Dollar Round Table and the President in 2002, Marv and Vicki represent MDRT all over the world. Marv's MDRT travel requirements are so extensive that insurance considerations preclude Vicki from serving as his pilot. So for the present they have sold her plane. Her flying days are not over—just on hold. They will purchase a new plane when Marv's commitments at MDRT are completed in 2003.

## ☘ Jerry and Melody Figurski

Jerry and Melody are very active, very involved individuals who are constantly on the go! They have so many interests—golf, tennis, football, volunteer activities, dancing, talking, story and joke telling, etc. Some of these activities they do with each other and others they do with friends. They each prefer the activities they do together.

Since moving to the warm Florida climate they have pretty much abandoned bridge. And, sharing the same side of the tennis court is not always fun. Both of them wanting so much to win for each other sometimes causes tension to rise and below par games to develop. Therefore, most of their tennis is scheduled with respective "guy friends" and "girl friends."

They do enjoy golf together. Melody plays a regular game with the women during the week and with Jerry on the weekends. Jerry opts to spend his weekend "golf time" with Melody instead of with the guys because they prefer to spend the time together. Jerry and Melody also love to make love. Lovemaking or sex can be, and is for them, a fulfilling part of married life. (If you listen to the TV talk shows you would think it has to end when you say, "I do.")

Jerry and Melody also enjoy just talking to each other! They love to share opinions and ideas and, of course, share their day's activities. They talk a lot about their volunteer work; work that is a major part of their lives. Though much

59

of their volunteering is done separately they totally support each other in all of it. They both participate in the constant array of events and social occasions connected with their volunteerism.

Perhaps their greatest interest and biggest passion is football. Melody has had football in her blood since her junior high cheerleading days and her days as a young girl learning the finer points of the game with her dad. She says she impressed many a college date with her knowledge of holding, grounding, and hang time.

Jerry and Melody moved to Florida in 1975, just after it was announced that an NFL franchise was coming to Tampa. They have been committed Buccaneer fans ever since. They have not missed a single home game in the 25 seasons! Actually, Melody and Jerry have each missed one game— but they were different games so between them they have been there for all of them! They are the epitome of true fans.

In fact, Melody is the Ultimate Buccaneer Fan. She was officially named the Ultimate Fan in 1999 at which time she was flown up to Canton, Ohio to be installed in the Football Hall of Fans at the Football Hall of Fame. Her name and picture were placed on the wall. Her name will be there forever.

Melody's undying support of the Buccaneers became even more meaningful during the 1992 season when she attended every home game while going through chemotherapy. She scheduled her chemo sessions around her tennis matches and the Bucs football games!

Jerry and Melody thrive on sharing their many interests and activities with family and friends. But above all, they thrive on sharing and being with each other. They are best friends.

## 🍀 Joe and Harriet Coren

Joe and Harriet's interests are not as extensive as some couples, but the interests they do share are very intense. As I mentioned earlier, their family is still among their primary interests even though the children have long left the "nest." Together they share phone calls, emails, and visits.

Another interest that deeply binds Joe and Harriet is their religion. They enjoy sharing their Jewish faith. They go to Temple together each week and celebrate holidays with Temple members. To them fellow Temple members are like family. However, going to Philadelphia to celebrate Passover with their daughter, Susie, and their son-in-law, Ken, is a must! The preparation for the celebration starts several days in advance with dad and Susie doing the cooking. The hustle and bustle in the kitchen with all the stories and the reminiscing is the start of the wonderful tradition. Often as many as 24 family members and friends join them at the seder table.

Volunteering in the local hospital is another activity that interests both of them. Joe puts in many more volunteer hours than Harriet does but, then, at 73 years of age, Harriet is still running her own secretarial business.

##  John Green and Susan Capio

John and Susan's interests are limited to their children these days. They say they gain their pleasure from watching their girls grow and learn and experience life. The simple joy of observing Michelle and Jennifer fills them with pride and love for their girls. Having had so much time together before starting their family makes them feel comfortable with the idea of putting couple interests on hold to focus on the family. My strong belief is that John and Susan need to make a greater effort to share time and interests with each other. They are losing the priority of the couple. The effects are already showing in their relationship. Sharing interests in common is very binding!

Interests are unique to each individual and to each individual couple. The point that must not be missed is that it is absolutely essential to develop some common interests to share. Sometimes it is not easy for two people to find the same interests, but it is critical to search for them. It is easier to bond and continue to bond with a person with whom you share interests. Some couples might feel their children provide the common interests, especially during their growing up years. While this is partially true, often what they are really sharing is "mutual concern," not common interests. Mutual concern does not quite fulfill the same role as common interests in strengthening a marriage.

## UNITY OF RELIGION

Unity of religion, or lack thereof, is an area more and more couples are dealing with today. There is a greater diversity of religion in cities, towns, and schools since the 60's. People are moving to different sections of the country and the world, and are taking their diverse religions with them. There is more likelihood today of connecting with someone with a different religious background. Although there seems to be more acceptance and flexibility where religion is concerned, there are still individuals, families, and social groups who have trouble understanding and accepting the beliefs of others.

When two people have been brought up with the same religious background—views, traditions, and customs—there is less of an adjustment for them as a couple and for extended family participation. Differences in religions, like differences in any other area, can cause additional challenges to a relationship. These challenges and decisions may start right at the beginning with decisions about the wedding service. What kind of a service should be held? Where? Who should officiate? Whose traditions and religion will be followed?

I have attended a number of interdenominational weddings in the last 20 to 30 years. Often with two diverse religions a civil ceremony is held. Last year I attended a wedding at which both a rabbi and a priest performed the ceremony in a dual service. It was beautiful!

There are additional challenges and decisions when children are brought into the picture. In what religion should the children be raised? Will the couple share both religions with the children and then let them choose?

There can be difficulties even when both spouses are basically brought up in the same religion. There are extremes and variations of interpretation even within the same religion.

### 🍀 Pat and Judy Siracusa

Pat and I were both Catholic when we met at college and still there were many differences in our religious beliefs and upbringing. My parents raised my brother and me Catholic, yet they did not practice the religion themselves.

Although my father had been raised Catholic, he pulled away from the church as an adult. He had been married briefly and divorced. This added to his distancing himself from the church. Divorce was not accepted in the Catholic religion. My mom was also born into the Catholic faith yet her father raised her as a single parent and did not practice the religion. Although my parents did not attend church themselves, they sent us kids to catechism classes and to church on Sundays. Pat's parents, on the other hand, strictly followed all the church's teachings. They lived in an Italian, Catholic neighborhood. All of Pat's friends and family were Catholic. He even attended a Catholic high school.

I lived in a small upper class town, Bronxville, NY. It was a white, Anglo-Saxon, Protestant community. I was one of only a very few Catholics and an Italian at that! It was a purely WASP neighborhood and, although I was well accepted by my friends, some of their families were not as accepting of me.

Sometimes I would go on weekend retreats with my friends' Protestant Church groups and be invited to share my Catholic views. I did this, though at the time I was questioning my own religious beliefs. In those days, the Catholic Church taught that non-Catholics could not enter heaven. It was difficult for me to accept the theory that all my friends, as well as my parents, would not be allowed into heaven.

I was definitely in search of another religion when I arrived at college. Meeting Pat, a devout Catholic, caused me to put a crashing halt to my religious search!

We were married in a Catholic ceremony, but did not have the traditional mass with the service. I am sure this was a bit distressing to Pat's much more religious family. Pat and I began to slowly pull away from the church not long after we married. However, when we visited Pat's parents or they visited us, we attended church. We did start to make more of an effort to attend church after we had children, but we were still not avid churchgoers.

After we moved to Florida we placed our children in a Catholic school because we felt the education was stronger than in the public schools there. This caused us to have greater contact with the church. As the boys were

65

growing up I became more and more committed to the Catholic religion.

Over the years the church's dogma has become a little more flexible and, therefore, a little more acceptable to me. Pat did not come back to the church as much as I did, but he does attend Sunday services with me—if it does not interfere with a tennis match or another more important activity.

Our boys, all grown now, have stopped attending church regularly. Our two married sons, Pat, Jr. and David and their wives, Kara and Fran, have stopped attending church. Although they were all brought up Catholic and married in the Catholic Church, they only attend mass on Christmas Eve with the family. They will all probably come back to the church when they have children. Children have a way of doing that to you! Raising children definitely increases one's need for a spiritual power.

## 🍀 Marvin and Vicki Feldman

Even though Marv and Vicki had very different religious backgrounds, religion has never been a problem for them as a couple or as a family. Marvin was brought up Jewish. Vicki was not brought up with any specific religious training. Although Vicki's father was a very spiritual man, he believed you should not have to "pay to pray." So growing up, Vicki and her family did not belong to any church.

The only challenge came from Marv's family's initial lack of acceptance of Vicki because she was not Jewish. Marv and Vicki are very cautious and thoughtful individuals so they made religious decisions for themselves and their girls with care and planning.  When they decided to get married, Vicki converted to Judaism primarily to please Marv's parents.  They  chose to raise the girls in one religion, Judaism.  As adults the girls have been made to feel comfortable making their own religious choices.  Barbi married a Christian man—while Terri's fiance is Jewish.

## 🍀 Jerry and Melody Figurski

The religious backgrounds of Jerry and Melody were very different.  Jerry was born and raised a Roman Catholic in a small Polish town where almost all activities revolved around the church.  He attended Catholic school until the eighth grade and was actively involved in the church.  He was an altar boy.  Melody was originally raised Catholic by her Irish Catholic mother, yet her upbringing was not at all similar to Jerry's.  First of all, although her mother was Irish Catholic, her father was the son of a Congregational minister.  Melody's parents did not always attend church with her unless they were visiting her father's parents and then they did not attend the Catholic Church, they went to her grandfather's Congregational Church.  So, despite the fact Melody attended mass and went to catechism, the message she received about religion was somewhat disconcerting.

It became even more confusing after her mother died of cancer.  Melody was only eleven years old.  Two years later her dad remarried a Protestant woman with three Protestant children.  At the age of thirteen, Melody not only acquired a new mother and three new siblings, she also got a new religion.  She began attending the Protestant Church on a regular basis with her new family.

Jerry and Melody married in the Congregational Church on the campus of Kent State University.  For some time Jerry had been questioning some issues with the Roman Catholic Church, such as Papal infallibility.  Both Jerry and Melody now feel a little regret at not having included a Catholic priest at their marriage ceremony for the sake of Jerry's family.

Through the years Jerry and Melody attended several churches.  After being married in the Congregational Church in Kent, they both became involved in guiding the high school youth group.

When they moved to Florida they began attending the downtown Clearwater Methodist Church until a new Methodist church opened in the Countryside area nearer their home.  They then began to feel the need for more liturgy, among other things, so they switched to an Episcopalian Mission church.  By the time their 25th wedding anniversary came around they had made a final move to the Catholic Church.  It was there that they renewed their marriage vows.

Jerry and Melody believe that through their exodus from one church to another they gained insight and compassion.  The same basic beliefs were reinforced in each of the various churches.  Their only possible regret was not choosing one faith for the religious stability of their children. Yet, their son, David, has turned out to be a very compassionate and loving person. Jerry and Melody believe strongly that David lives the life God wants him to live. David is a very concerned and caring young man. He is always willing to help family, friends, and acquaintances. He married Melissa, a young woman with a strong Lutheran background. They have joined a Lutheran Church in Austin, Texas where they now live. Hopefully, David and Melissa will feel com-fortable in their church and will, together, be able to raise their children in a stable religious community.

## 🍀 Joe and Harriet Coren

Joe and Harriet were born into the same religion, but when they met in 1945 Joe was not a practicing Jew. The last time he had been in a Synagogue was when he had his Bar Mitzvah ten years earlier.

Joe and Harriet met at a dance at the "Y" that was given for the returning service men. Joe had just been dis-charged from two long years in Europe. They met and danced together all evening.

Joe asked Harriet to go out with him on the Friday night following the Sunday night dance. Harriet said she was going to Synagogue and if he wanted to come along she would go out with him afterward. Harriet had a strong commitment to her religion. She will be the first one to tell you they worked out their religious differences because, as usual, Joe went along with her choices. They had a

Jewish wedding and Joe and Harriet have been dancing and praying together ever since!

For their 50th anniversary three years ago they had a beautiful renewal of their vows in Synagogue.  Their son, Buzz, walked them down the aisle.  Their daughter, Susie and son-in-law, Ken, and grandchildren, Adena and Yoni, held the traditional canopy.  It was as meaningful as their first ceremony—maybe even more so!

##  John Green and Susan Capio

John is Jewish.  Susan is Catholic.  While neither of them was especially devout when they met and married, neither of them wanted to convert, either.  They decided to maintain their separate religions and believed they would also let their children make their own choices when the time came.  However, the decisions about their girls' religions were continually postponed until their oldest daughter turned five years old.  Religion had become a very touchy subject.

When John and Susan first got married they had the idealistic view that they could raise their children in both religions, since as a couple, this worked for them.  What they began to realize, as their oldest daughter started to ask pointed questions, was that she needed to know "who she was."  They realized then that they must provide her with a base of knowledge so she could begin developing her spiritual side.  It would be too confusing to teach her both religions. They decided if they, as adults, could not decide on one religion; it would surely be too difficult for her.

After much debate and a number of meetings with both clergy, it came down to which parent took charge. Mom took control. Both girls are presently being brought up in the Catholic religion. It was a decision they hoped would work. It still remains an unresolved issue.

Religious issues can become a major challenge if both spouses do not agree upon the resolution of these issues. The four "lucky" couples worked out their religious differences satisfactorily because of their commitment to each other and their family. They did it together.

John and Susan are still struggling with their religious differences because Susan took control of the girls' religion and John is still not comfortable with the situation. Susan is quick to take charge—often before mutual solutions are agreed upon.

## UNITY IN OTHER AREAS

## ENVIRONMENT

Another area to explore is environment.  Do you like to live in the city or the country?  Do you like big towns or small towns? Do you like a cold climate or a warm climate or a climate with changing seasons?  Environment can become an issue if there are extremes in the couple's desires.

## 🍀 Pat and Judy Siracusa

Pat and I are definitely warm weather people.  We love the year round sunshine in Florida, the sunshine state.  We have never for a moment doubted our choice of the warm climate. We even like the hot, humid summers. The weather in Florida is conducive to the sporting activities we most enjoy—tennis, biking, and golf.  And, although we love to ski, one or two weeks in the cold mountains of Colorado are enough for us.

## 🍀 Marvin and Vicki Feldman

Marv and Vicki grew up in a small town in the cold north-east.  However, due to their extensive travels they have never had to feel too limited by the area they called "home." They were always flying and visiting all parts of the United States and abroad.  They also had a permanent place to stay in Florida to escape from the cold weather if they chose. Having built a lovely home a few years ago on Lake Tarpon in Florida now allows them to spend even more time in the warm climate. Vicki loves the warm weather. Marv feels Florida's heat is a little much at times. Fortunately they do have the freedom to move about and make changes.

## 🍀 Jerry and Melody Figurski

Environmental choices for the Figurski's were more about family than about weather or area. Their move from Ohio to Florida was made primarily to be near Melody's parents. They both, however, appreciate the warm weather and sunny skies. Actually, before Jerry met Melody he had hardly ventured out of the state of Ohio.

After they married they made a number of trips to Florida. On each trip Melody's mom would have a job interview ready for Jerry. In 1975 he took the interview and accepted a position at the Pinellas County Attorney's office. They made the move.

They enjoy the weather, business opportunities, and extensive involvement in numerous organizations and activities in the Tampa Bay community. The distance the move put between Jerry and his extended family is the only downside.

## 🍀 Joe and Harriet Coren

In the winter of 1969 Joe decided cold weather and shoveling snow were not for him anymore.  Joe and Harriet moved to Florida in the winter of 1970 where the temperature on Christmas Day was a balmy 75 degrees!  While Harriet quickly adjusted to the climate, she still felt she should pack for her return trip home.  She eventually came to understand she was not on vacation.  The warm weather, sunny skies, and beautiful beaches were "home!"

## 💔 John Green and Susan Capio

John and Susan have made the transition from the very warm state of Florida to the cold northeast and finally back south.  The weather is not as much an issue with them as the living arrangements.

John cherishes a home and a yard he can be proud of.  He loves "yard work."  He enjoys being at home puttering around or simply watching TV.

Susan, on the other hand, has never really felt the same attachment to a house.  She likes to live in a nice place, but is more concerned with being on the go and doing things.  Their girls can share the comforts of home with dad and be out and about with mom.

## PETS

Pets can be another source of issues. One spouse may love animals, while the other spouse, may not even like them. Or worse yet, he or she may be allergic to them.

### ❦ Pat and Judy Siracusa

Pat and I bought our first pet within weeks after our wedding. Pat was not allowed to have any pets growing up, so he was determined to get one as soon as we were married. Our German Shepherd, Mister PE, was an important part of our life during our first years together. He was our baby. He was a loving and faithful dog, but unfortunately, his extremely protective nature toward us forced us to give him away when we were expecting our first child.

Through the years as our children were growing up we had several pets that provided us with years of stories and laughter. We had fish, hamsters, cats, and dogs. Some of the cats were well accepted by the family, while others had to struggle to survive. We had one special dog, Flash, who we all loved the most. Flash was a good natured, lazy, loving basset/beagle mutt that died more than 18 years ago and, yet, he still sparks many family discussions.

After our youngest son, Brian, left for college, I wanted to fill the "empty nest" with a pet. Pat nixed my plan. He said, "We have our freedom now, why hamper it?" We have been "empty nesters" for awhile and he was right. It is fun enjoying the freedom of picking up and going whenever we desire.

## 2 Marvin and Vicki Feldman

Marv has always enjoyed having pets in the family. Vicki probably likes them even more. Sometimes she goes overboard caring for her pets. One example is the night their Dalmatian was in need of extra affection, so she let the dog into bed with her . . . and Marv! The Dalmatian proceeded to "drop a load" in the bed. Vicki did not want Marv to find out what the dog had done so she attempted to change the sheets—while Marv slept! As far as Marv was concerned that should have been the poor dumb Dalmatian's last night as a Feldman. As it happened, the dog was around for a long time.

Today Vicki and Marv just have a cat. Vicki is anxious to get another dog (not a Dalmatian) but she has agreed to wait until they are through with the extensive demands of MDRT travel.

## 3 Jerry and Melody Figurski

Jerry and Melody were given the only pet they have ever owned by Melody's parents. They both loved her parents' poodle and obviously expressed that love enough times to prompt the Wordsworths into surprising them with a poodle of their own the Christmas before they had their first child! They had never even thought about owning a pet nor do they ever choose to own one again. Yet, they did cherish their dog, Snap, for the 18 years she was with them and their kids.

## 🍀 Joe and Harriet Coren

Joe and Harriet always had pets while their children were growing up—the usual—and the not so usual! One of their dogs that fit into the "not so usual" group was their little toy fox terrier. Fox terriers are known to be smart, but this one was at the top of the class. The Hebrew word for dog is "kelev" so they named their terrier "Keli" Joe and Harriet spoke to Keli in English while their children, Susie and Buzz, chose to speak to him in Hebrew. He was bilingual!

Other interesting pets included three baby raccoons Buzz brought home because their mom had been a road-kill. In order to save the babies, the whole family had to pitch in for the night feedings. They color coordinated the process. Each raccoon had painted nails to match their colored bottle. It worked!

Another family pet project involved the incubation of fertile chicken eggs. Each family member was assigned a shift to turn the eggs every six hours. Of the 24 eggs, 18 produced successful embryos that were sealed in jars of formaldehyde. Buzz donated them to the science lab at his school. They are still on display 30 years later!

##  John Green and Susan Capio

John Green and Susan Capio have never been pet owners. While he was growing up, John had a dog, Sport, that he loved. As a result, he has always wanted to get a dog for the girls, but Susan feels it would be too inconvenient with business, family and their numerous moves.

## GOALS AND DREAMS

Unity of goals and dreams is important. Goals and dreams can vary greatly and unless they are discussed and understood, they can become major issues. One spouse may dream of a life of wealth and power, while the other spouse may desire a life filled with family, creative projects, and fun-filled recreation.

Things change. Goals are often adjusted throughout a lifetime. Sometimes circumstances will cause individuals to reconsider the direction of their lives. Recently, a young woman told me that her husband had a near death experience with cancer. The challenges he faced and his difficult recovery gave him a whole new perspective on his life. He has had to re-establish his priorities!

## 🍀 Pat and Judy Siracusa

Pat and I have modified our goals and dreams throughout our life together. These were not extreme changes, as much as they were "time frame" changes. We never formalized our goals and dreams before marriage. We are not the analytical types. Things just evolve for us.

Initially our education decided our career paths. Teaching was an upstanding, well thought of profession in our families. The lack of financial gain from teaching was not an issue in the beginning because we were doing better financially than our parents. We bought a home in a nice middle class neighborhood. Our friends from school and our neighbors were all in the same economic bracket. We had a home, acceptable furnishings, and a fun life. We were very cautious with our spending. We had to be.

We eventually had three children and just one teacher's salary to live on because I had become a stay-at-home mom. Going out to dinner once a year was a real splurge! One annual weekend get-away at a nearby inexpensive resort was our extravagance. We had friends with whom we shared time and activities as couples. And, of course, we spent lots of time with our children.

We camped with our children and our friends, biked, played tennis, shared dinners, cooked out in our backyard, and enjoyed a number of low cost activities. We lived content- edly within our means. It was a good, conservative life.

Winters did get long. Tennis was becoming a good money- maker for Pat. Pat's roommate from college, Al Morris, had moved to Florida and insisted it was the ideal place for us to live. When we took our chance and made the move to Florida it opened up a whole new world for us. And, I do not mean just the sunny skies and warm tem- peratures. Working at the country club exposed us to a completely different lifestyle than we were accustomed to. Our new friends and new activities were different than back home. Dining at nice restaurants, vacationing at beautiful resorts, driving expensive cars, owning nice homes, etc., were the norm for our new group.

As we got a taste of the "good life" we wanted more and more of it. We raised our goals and dreams in the financial rewards department. Material things have never been a huge priority with us and that has not changed much. We are still fairly conservative with money—I much more than Pat. But, there is a tremendous difference between what we considered conservative as teachers and what we consider conservative today.

## 🍀 Marvin and Vicki Feldman

With most people things happen and life just seems to evolve. This is not the case with Marv and Vicki. Yes, there have been changes in their lives, but not without extensive forethought and planning. They do not make major life decisions impulsively. Actually, they do not make any decisions impulsively—except when purchasing art.

Marv and Vicki hold the same goals and dreams. They developed them years ago and together have continued to live them. They have gone through different stages of development, focus, and passage, but the basics remain ever constant. Love and care for family, success in business, and enjoyment of life have always been their priorities. They are truly of one mind and one heart. They always have been and always will be!

## 🍀 Jerry and Melody Figurski

Jerry and Melody did not formulate grandiose goals, dreams, or life plans before they married in 1967. Thinking back to what they hoped for, it would probably have simply been a happy life with a happy family, good friends, and challenging careers.  The careers they envisioned were careers in education.  They both loved the university community and thrived on teaching while continuing their own education.

One of Jerry's desires was to obtain a Masters degree  and then a Ph.D.  Jerry switched from teaching 6th and 8th grades to teaching college. To his surprise he found that he did not enjoy teaching on the college level as much as he had the middle school level.

Melody originally started out pursuing a career in business. Within a few years she realized she should have taken the education courses that her advisors had recommended.  So in 1969 she started taking some educational courses while she taught adult education classes.  She continued teaching adult business courses part time until 1983 while Jerry was getting his law degree and building his law practice.

During this time of teaching and studying Jerry and Melody bought their first home.  It was 1,100 sq. ft. and cost $23,000.  Jerry told Melody this was just the beginning  some day he would buy her a $50,000 house! Melody's reply was, "Oh, Jerry, we'll never have a $50,000 home, but that's not what's important."  In truth, in the 60's a $50,000 home was a pretty far reach for a teacher. Melody believed that the important things in life were not material things. What was important was to be happy with family and friends.

Things change.  Following the tragedy of Kent State in 1970 and Jerry's lessening enthusiasm with teaching he decided to change his focus to law. Instead of working on a doctoral degree in education he started law school. It was a time consuming, stressful undertaking, but with Melody's complete support he achieved his new goal.

Melody married a hard working, successful teacher and ended up with a hard working, very successful lawyer. Jerry's promise of a $50,000 home has been far exceeded. Their economic lifestyle is very different from what they envisioned back in the 60's.

Another event that changed their lives forever was the birth of their first child. Nine days after Tracy was born they were faced with a parent's worst nightmare. Their daughter was diagnosed as brain damaged. Things could never be the way they had expected after that.

They still wanted another child. It was a big decision. Three-and-a-half years later their son, David, was born. He was healthy, happy and for them, the "perfect" child! He is bright, athletic, and extremely loving. He has added so much to their lives.

Tracy has also added a lot to their lives. Her disabilities have been very difficult and life altering, yet she has taught them a great deal. Her eagerness to please, her loving nature, and her ability to have fun have been very heart warming.

Melody had planned to be a stay-at-home mother. After Tracy was born there was no doubt she would always be needed to stay at home, so any goals of pursuing a full

time career were put on hold forever.  As mentioned ex-
tensively in the first chapter, Melody has used time away
from the home to do an enormous amount of volunteer
work in the community.  Volunteerism was something she
could fit in around Tracy's schedule.

Jerry and Melody did not set lofty goals when they were
first married.  They wanted simply to have a happy life with
family and friends.  Yes, unplanned things happened in their
lives.  Their daughter, Tracy, was born with disabilities.  This
made them even more dedicated to their children.   Their
son, David, was born "perfect." Both children have made
them proud and happy.

Jerry changed careers from teaching to law.  This put them
in a financial position they never could have expected.
Through challenge and change they have achieved the
"American Dream"—a happy family, good friends, and
challenging careers.

## 🍀 Joe and Harriet Coren

Joe and Harriet had the occasion to take a long hard
look at their goals and dreams following their close en-
counter on December 25, 1975.  They were hit broad-
side on U.S. 19 in Clearwater, Florida by a car speeding
through a red light.  Joe took the full impact breaking all
of his ribs on his left side, puncturing a lung and receiving massive head wounds.  He was in the hospital for
two months.

Although Harriet went through the windshield and side window she did not sustain nearly the injuries Joe did. Joe and Harriet have not reestablished their priorities, they are just ever more grateful for the blessed lives they are living.

##  John Green and Susan Capio

John and Susan may have started out with the same goals and dreams, but through the years their goals have definitely evolved in different directions. Once they started their family, John became more focused and committed to the girls than to his aspirations in the business world. Susan, although she loves the girls, has not lost her passion and drive to succeed in business. She is a driven individual.

❁❁❁

Goals and dreams usually change through the course of a lifetime. This is quite natural and is likely to happen because things do not stay the same—they develop and evolve. Hopefully, these changes develop and evolve with both spouses in sync.

> ❁❁❁ *It is important to have similar goals and dreams* ❁❁❁

There are so many spectrums to be explored under the "U" in a lucky marriage. However, it is the couple's unity of spirit, oneness of heart, and commitment that sets the stage for a "lucky" marriage.

Here is a checklist for the "U":

## CHECKLIST FOR THE "U"

__1. THE MORE AREAS OF UNITY IN THE MAR-RIAGE, THE MORE CHANCE FOR A "LUCKY" MARRIAGE.

__2. IT IS IMPORTANT TO MAINTAIN UNITY OF SPIRIT, HEART, AND COMMITMENT.

__3. MAKE YOUR RELATIONSHIP A PRIORITY.

__4. THE UNITY OF THE COUPLE ESTABLISHES THE STRENGTH OF THE FAMILY.

__5. DO NOT HAVE CHILDREN IN ORDER TO TRY TO MAKE YOUR MARRIAGE STRONGER.

__6. DO NOT LET CHILDREN BECOME YOUR ONLY AREA OF UNITY.

__7. MAKE TIME FOR EACH OTHER.

__8. MAKE TIME AND EFFORT TO DEVELOP UNITY WITH EXTENDED FAMILY.

__9.    DEVELOP INTERESTS TOGETHER
        AS A COUPLE.

__10.   ESTABLISH YOUR RELIGIOUS RITUALS,
        TRADITIONS, AND PRACTICES.

__11.   AGREE ON HAVING OR NOT
        HAVING PETS.

__12.   DECIDE ON AN ACCEPTABLE
        ENVIRONMENT.

__13.   FOCUS ON GOALS, DREAMS,
        AND DESIRES.

__14.   SUCCESSFUL MARRIAGES
        CAN EXIST EVEN IF THERE
        IS NOT UNITY IN ALL AREAS.

# CHAPTER THREE

## "C"

## "C" Stands for Communication

Good communication is crucial to a "lucky" marriage. It is a necessary part of any relationship! Unfortunately, the ability to communicate effectively is not a part of many marriages. Lack of effective communication is a large contributing factor to the high numbers of nonfunctioning marriages and/or divorces.

Communication is the ability to share thought and feeling in order to promote mutual understanding. So often, especially in today's busy world, we do not take the time to communicate. Time is a key factor in communicating effectively.

Many couples do not take time, or rather, do not make time to communicate with each other. You might conclude there is not enough time in this rushed world to just sit and talk. Well, it goes back to the issue of priorities. A couple must take the time to communicate. It is vital to a healthy marriage.

❀❀❀ *Make time to communicate* ❀❀❀

89

Communication is the key to keeping things on course.  It is the key to keeping the many challenges of marriage and family at a manageable level.  Good communication with our spouse can keep the couple relationship and the family functioning.  Good communication will help to keep our fast paced lives under control.  And, it is vital to establish a strong system for communication right from the start.  When the challenges of life turn into frustration and stress, the first thing to go is communication.

*❀❀❀ Strong communication*
*with mutual understanding*
*is key to a "lucky" marriage ❀❀❀*

Communication is a simple process of sending and receiving messages.  Yet, so often one message is sent and a very different message is received.  In order for the simple circle of communication to be completed a message must be sent and that same message must be received and then fed back.  Amazingly the full cycle is completed less than 70% of the time!  Let's take a look at why this simple cycle of communication is so often not completed.

Listening is the key.  Or, rather, not listening is the key!  So many of us worked on communication skills either in school or in the business environment.  We worked on reading skills, presentation skills, and writing skills.  But, how many worked on developing our listening skills?  I would guess not many!  In order for the message to be received we must learn to listen and hear the entire message sent.  Words are only 7% of communication.  That means we must listen not only with our ears, but our eyes, our brains, and our hearts as well.

*❀❀❀ Listening is the first*
*and most important step*
*in the communication process ❀❀❀*

The first key to good listening is to give the speaker our full attention. Yet, often when someone is trying to send us a message we are not paying attention. We are not listening at all. Rather, we are reading the newspaper or putting things away or doing some activity other than listening. Sometimes we just do not have the time or the patience to listen at the time our spouse chooses. If this is the case, perhaps we are in a hurry and simply cannot take the time to listen, then we must set aside a time when we will be able to listen. Schedule time as you would schedule time to exercise, or read, or do any other activity that is important to you. Set the time immediately. It can be at the next meal or during free time on the upcoming weekend. Just make sure you set the time and then do it!

*❀❀❀ Set the time to communicate ❀❀❀*

The listener may not receive the message even when time is set to communicate. Sometimes when you truly think you are listening, you are not. You may be analyzing what the person is saying; judging whether or not you agree or disagree with the information. Or worse yet, you may be developing your own rebuttal statement. You must listen first to understand the message your spouse is sending. Only after you are sure you fully understand what has been

91

expressed should you proceed with the communication process. Communication is for mutual understanding.

*✿✿✿ Communication is for*
*mutual understanding ✿✿✿*

Most of us go through life not realizing how poorly we communicate. Rarely do we even think about our inability to communicate. Only when major problems occur do we give it some thought. And yet, it is so important. It is an issue that must be addressed.

Why do people have such poor communication skills and what can be done to improve them? If listening is the major barrier to the communication process what can be done to improve it?

We must first make sure we are receiving the message the sender is sending. A wonderful technique for doing this is reflective listening. Reflective listening means feeding back the message being sent to you; the whole message, the words, the emotions, the entire message. It does not mean asking questions, giving opinions or telling stories that will top theirs. It means simply feeding back. "So as I understand it . . ." "What I'm hearing you say is . . ." It is a practice of repeating both the words and the feelings to be sure you have received the intended message. Practicing the skill of reflective listening is an important part of my training programs on communication. If it is the only skill they acquire during my program, it will be very worthwhile. It will significantly improve their communications skills.

92

*✿✿✿ Use reflective listening to be sure
you get the whole message ✿✿✿*

Of course most people say, "The problem is not about me not listening to my spouse, the problem is about getting my spouse to listen to me!" How do we get our spouse to listen to us? People listen to what is important to them. People will listen to things that have a direct effect on them. So if you want your spouse to listen to you, it is important to let them know that what you have to say affects them. People also listen better when you make them feel important. Individuals need to feel special. Everyone likes to feel important. Your spouse is no different. Make it a point to let your spouse know how important he or she is. One very simple way to make someone feel important is simply to listen! By listening you are telling the other person that you care enough to really hear what that person is saying.

After I do a reflective listening exercise in my programs I ask the participants how they felt during the exercise. Those doing the listening always say they have never listened so closely! In order to reflect both the words and the feelings they must listen intently. The ones doing the talking always say they feel important because someone is listening to them so carefully. They feel like the person listening really cares to hear what they are saying. They say they feel great. They feel special. They feel listened to! Some participants say they actually feel uncomfortable because they are not accustomed to having anyone listen to them so intently.

Listen to what your spouse has to say. Make your spouse feel special. Try to listen just to understand. Be there for him or her. It will end up being a wonderful gift for both of you because it will increase your ability to communicate and understand each other.

*✿✿✿ Listen*
*It will make your spouse feel specia l✿✿✿*

Good communication is such an extremely important part of a "lucky" marriage. Many of the things I spoke of in previous chapters have a strong effect on the couple's willingness and ability to communicate. Take the first Chapter about "Like." If you like someone you tend to try to communicate with him or her effectively. When you do not like someone you tend not to listen. By merely listening to your partner you are showing you like and love them.

The other very important issue connected with communication is making time to communicate. This reflects back to Chapter Two on "Unity." Couple priority means making time for your spouse. Always make couple time no matter what else is going on in your life. Interests in common also tie in with the issue of communication. If you develop common interests you will naturally spend more time together allowing more time for communicating.

Some couples communicate frequently, but also ineffectively. My parents spent hours and hours communicating in loud, negative shouting sessions. They developed a shouting communication style. I do not think they even

94

realized they were doing it. We get caught up in habits of acting and reacting. Sometimes we are not aware of the negative habits we develop. Habits are a way of life that can only be changed through being made aware of them and making a sincere effort to change.

Other couples deliberately do not communicate. They do not wish to cause waves. They consciously keep things from their spouse because they do not see the necessity or have the desire to share everything.

Some people develop the art of pretending—pretending things are fine. This may work for awhile for some couples, but these are not couples with truly "lucky" marriages. Couples with "lucky" marriages are more comfortable sharing things with their spouse than they are sharing with any other person. They communicate frequently and effectively.

## 🍀 Pat and Judy Siracusa

Pat and I have always been fairly strong in the area of communication. Through the years we have learned to communicate even more effectively with each other. Each of us tries to please the other.

Keeping peace and maintaining a state of happiness is very important to us. Neither of us likes conflict, so we work on keeping upbeat as much as possible. This, in itself, is not a bad thing, but it probably created barriers to more effective communication in the early years of our marriage. The fear of causing conflict or making any waves sometimes kept us from expressing our true feelings.

As an example, in the "U" Chapter I explained how lack of couple time and time spent away from our first born son came to a frustrating head for us one evening. The frustration would not have reached that point if I had shared my feelings of entrapment with Pat sooner. Things rarely build up between Pat and me anymore because we are more willing to communicate our feelings. We each truly care to hear and understand what the other one is thinking and feeling.  Of course, with the boys grown and gone and only the two of us at home, there is far less stress in our lives, less for us to have conflict over. The other reason we communicate more effectively is because we have been together so long.

## 🍀 Marvin and Vicki Feldman

Communication has never been a major challenge for Marv and Vicki, but they both agree this is an area they have improved upon over time.  In the beginning of their relationship Vicki had more trouble communicating effectively than Marv.

Vicki is the type of person who desires all things to remain calm at all times.  She hates to "rock the boat."  So, in order not to cause any disruptions in the early years she would attempt to hide her feelings.  Instead of expressing herself she would go into another room and shut the door.

Marv, on the other hand, has always believed the best way to deal with a difficult situation or a problem is to discuss it. Marv has helped Vicki learn to express herself and share her feelings even when she is uncomfortable with them.

Vicki communicates much more openly now. She can express herself before things become too difficult. Marv believes that the best way to deal with a situation is to confront it openly and honestly before it becomes a problem. This has really paid off for them.

The comfort level Marv and Vicki have achieved in their communication through the years is more than most couples even come close to experiencing. They are so much "in tune" that some times they find themselves talking for each other. They call it, "Marv talking Vicki" or "Vicki talking Marv."

## 🍀 Jerry and Melody Figurski

In many ways Jerry and Melody feel they are good communicators. They are both very verbal. Some of their most enjoyable times are spent just talking. They talk freely and often for fun and relaxation. However, sometimes on minor issues when little annoyances need to be unraveled, they get frustrated with each other's reactions.

The interesting aspect of their relationship is that they can handle big challenges when they are confronted with them—a developmentally disabled child?—cancer? No problem! Their love and determination allows them to weather these storms.  A minor flap and Jerry wants to "clam up."  Melody wants to resolve it now.  Jerry readily admits, on a logical level, that Melody's approach is better, but that does not always keep him from hoping things will just go away.

Relationships are so unique.  Jerry and Melody have needed extraordinary communication skills to get through so many challenges, many more challenges than most couples must endure in a lifetime.  Yet, communicating on what seems to be minor issues for most other couples has been their biggest relationship challenge.

## 🍀 Joe and Harriet Coren

Harriet likes to brag that she and Joe have never had an argument.  This is because Harriet argues and Joe does not.  Harriet stops talking only when Harriet tires of listening to Harriet!

She says Joe is so easy going that along the course of their lives together she must have coaxed him into doing many things that made him miserable.  Through the years she believes she has become more aware of his feelings and emotions.  She tries to stop to think more about what Joe wants.

A forceful person like Harriet who is quick to make decisions and a more reserved, giving person like Joe, sometimes find it difficult to adjust to each other.   However, because Harriet likes and respects Joe so much she knows it is important to understand and appreciate his wants and needs.

## ❤ John Green and Susan Capio

John and Susan need to increase their ability to communicate more effectively with each other. Through the years, especially the more recent years, they have been negligent in taking the time to communicate. At the beginning of their relationship the need for intense communication was not as vital. There were just the two of them. They would be content to come and go in many different directions—often pursuing their own activities. This worked for them and might have continued working if they did not have children.

In their case the children have become the only shared focus of their life together. Interests and couple time have been put on hold. This has cut down their time for effective and meaningful communication. Since the girls have come into their lives they are not only busier, but also focused in different directions. Communication is almost non-existent. Things will only get worse if they do not make a very conscious effort to work on communicating more. The only way to know what the other is thinking and feeling is to share these thoughts and emotions with each other. John and Susan do not do this!

Strong, effective communication is so important to a good relationship. Many problems could be eliminated with a strong communication system. When couples go to a marriage counselor one of the main things the counselor works on is improving the couple's communication. When stress or challenges build up in any relationship the very first thing to break down is communication. Therefore, it is necessary to develop a strong communication system as soon as possible.

Here is a checklist for the "C":

## CHECKLIST FOR THE "C"

__1.  COMMUNICATION TAKES TIME.
       MAKE TIME!

__2.  COMMUNICATION IS FOR MUTUAL
       UNDERSTANDING.

__3.  GIVE YOUR SPOUSE YOUR
       FULL ATTENTION.

__4.  LISTEN NOT JUST WITH YOUR
       EARS, BUT YOUR EYES, HEART,
       AND BRAIN.

__5.  LISTEN TO UNDERSTAND,
       NOT TO JUDGE.

__6.  LISTEN TO THE ENTIRE
       MESSAGE SENT.

__7.   USE REFLECTIVE LISTENING.


__8.   UNDER PRESSURE AND STRESS
       THE FIRST THING TO GO IS
       THE ABILITY TO COMMUNICATE
       EFFECTIVELY.


__9.   LISTENING SAYS, "I CARE."

## CHAPTER FOUR

## "K"

### "K" Stands for Kisses, Hugs, and More

Marriage is not a simple institution. There are many aspects to married life. Some parts of marriage involve necessary activities that are mundane and routine. There are the business aspects, the housekeeping aspects, family ties, work, special interests, etc. During the courting period and when the wedding bells are still ringing in our ears there seems to be no limit to the lovemaking, the kissing, hugging, and other shows of affection.

However, as time rolls along, the honeymoon becomes ancient history and the daily routine becomes "ho-hum." The show of affection may become a forgotten part of the relationship. You cannot let this happen if you want to maintain a "lucky" marriage. You must keep the fun and enthusiasm alive by making an effort to always include "Kisses, Hugs, and More!"

There are many ways to display affection. Lovemaking is one of those ways. And, contrary to what you hear on many talk shows, lovemaking or sex does not have to die after marriage! For some couples it may become a little more difficult to maintain the excitement. And, it can be even more of a challenge to find the time for lovemaking when children come into the picture. But, like making time to share interests in common or making time to communicate, it is necessary to make time for lovemaking. Lovemaking is part of the marriage commitment. It should be not only honored, but also enjoyed. It definitely helps keep the couple relationship alive.

*❁❁❁ Lovemaking should be
an enjoyable part of marriage ❁❁❁*

Now there is a lot more to "Kisses, Hugs, and More" than just lovemaking or sex. Shows of affection can be done in so many special ways. Kisses are good. Hugs are comforting. A touch, a knowing smile, a look of approval, a hand held, or a wink of the eye all contribute to a feeling of closeness.

"Kisses, Hugs, and More" essentially include everything spouses do for each other to express their love and caring. The difference I see between couples with "lucky" marriages and couples with marriages that are just "functioning" is that a spouse in a "lucky" marriage does these special things because of the joy it brings to his or her mate. In a "functioning" marriage the show of affection to a mate is out of obligation—a means to keep the spouse content enough to keep the marriage "functioning."

Much of "Kisses, Hugs, and More" is simply having awareness and consideration of your spouse. Being perceptive, caring how your spouse is doing and feeling. Always be there. Giving your spouse praise is another extremely important part of "Kisses, Hugs, and More."

When you notice something positive in how your spouse looks or what he or she has done, express it. So many couples get caught in the unfortunate habit of speaking up only when there is a point of criticism or correction to be made. It is more important to praise than to contradict or criticize. Many couples who get into a rut of complaining and criticizing are unaware they have developed such a pattern. It is so easy to find fault and so much more important to praise. Praise can do so much for a relationship!

*❀❀❀ It is always important*
*to praise your spouse ❀❀❀*

There are so many other ways you can show your spouse you are thinking about him or her. You can buy a special gift, prepare a favorite meal, write a loving note, send flowers, undertake a project that your spouse considers important, or simply listen when your spouse needs you to do so. Listening and empathizing are worth thousands of kisses and hugs.

## 🍀 Pat and Judy Siracusa

Pat is always commenting on how well I look in a particular outfit, how trim I am, or how pretty I look on a given day. He is so sincere in his compliments that he makes me feel good about myself. I, in turn, cannot keep from telling him how great he looks or how upbeat he is or how much fun I have with him. We say, "I love you" spontaneously and often. It might sound "gooey," but it is sincere and natural with us.

As I am writing this chapter, Pat is in San Francisco for a week at a Million Dollar Round Table Convention. Each day while he is gone he has his secretary give me one of the gifts he bought before he left. I have received a night-shirt, bathing suit cover-up, belt, and flowers. What a way to keep our relationship alive! He is always doing little things like this—more than I do. He loves to shop. I shop because we need things. A couple of months ago I happened to mention that my roasting pan "had seen its day." A few days later he showed up with a new pan that he bought on his way home from work. This is definitely a part of "Kisses, Hugs, and More."

Another way Pat shows his love for me is by stopping by McDonald's to buy me a cup of coffee. I love McDonald's coffee. On the way to the office in the morning I swing through "Mickey D's" for a large cup of coffee, one cream. It is my wake up call. On weekends sometimes I just want to hang out in the morning and Pat will make a run to McDonald's and bring home some coffee for me. He does not even drink it—it is just for me. When we are on a road trip, Pat will take the time to swing by the drive-through for my morning cup of coffee. I really appreciate it! This is part of "Kisses, Hugs, and More."

Although I do not shower Pat with gifts, I often write him cards or notes expressing my love. I also try to take care of his needs at home. Our division of work is very much from the old school of husband/wife duties. Since I was a longtime stay-at-home mom, I have always been in charge of the household chores.

My goal is to serve Pat when he is at home. He is an incredibly hard worker, putting in long office hours. Putting together dinners he enjoys and serving him is part of my "Kisses, Hugs, and More." He has always been the breadwinner in our family. Although I now run my own business, the pressure of financially supporting the family remains his. I am in charge of taking care of the home, the laundry, shopping, etc. He helps out sometimes now, but it remains my responsibility. This is the way we do it. It works for us.

Another way I show my love for Pat is by getting involved with some extra activities he really likes. One thing Pat has always enjoyed is biking. I did not dislike it; but I was never really into it. This year while I was at AAA scheduling some flight arrangements I inquired about biking tours. I was given a great brochure for Vermont Bike Tours. I selected a few trips that fit into our schedule and brought them home to Pat. We selected one and signed up! Then we began riding together each week to train. We enjoyed one of the best vacations we have ever had biking together for five days in beautiful Vermont. A biking trip in the hills of Vermont, especially considering we live in the flat lands of Florida, would not normally be my first choice for a fun vacation, but I knew how much this adventure would mean to Pat. I did it for Pat, part of my "Kisses, Hugs, and More," and I now enjoy biking, too. We have added it to our list of weekly activities.

## 🍀 Marvin and Vicki Feldman

Marv and Vicki are perfect examples of how "Kisses, Hugs, and More" are used to keep a relationship alive. You just have to be with them a short while to know they are a caring, loving couple. And, I do not mean because they are fawning or falling all over each other. Although from what they shared with me, I guess this was a concern of their girls when they were teenagers. They cautioned dad and mom not to embarrass them with a PDA (Public Display of Affection) when their friends came to visit. It has been a standing joke in their home for years.

I have never observed any outrageous PDA from Marv and Vicki. What I do observe is a lot of love and affection. You feel the vibes in the way they look at each other and react to each other. There is a strong sense of connection.

When they are at home alone they do like to be near each other, often sitting together reading or watching TV. They enjoy being close. They exchange a touch on the knee or a pat on the head. But Marv and Vicki are also fine watching TV in separate rooms if they want to watch different programs. Basically, they are totally and completely comfortable with each other.

Doing things for one another comes naturally to them. "Thinking" and "doing" for one another is a regular part of their day. They just do it—changing the electric toothbrush for each other, adjusting the memory buttons in the car, or bringing home a needed item. Vicki calls Marv's office to check if he needs anything and Marv does the same for Vicki on his way home. When Marv comes home from a long day at the office he does the dishes for Vicki. He says, "She cooks me a great meal, I can do the dishes." They enjoy being together and doing things for each other.

Other shows of affection include flowers sent to say, "I love you." Marv also enjoys sending crazy cards, some of which are dirty. Vicki loves receiving them! When business travel keeps them apart they try to stay in touch. Vicki often slips a note into Marv's suitcase. Marv sends flowers. They are always finding new ways to express how much they care.

Million Dollar Round Table is one of the conventions Marv attends each year that spouses are usually not invited to attend. In 2002, Marv will be the president of MDRT, the international organization of life insurance agents. Vicki always sends a basket of fruit to Marv's room before his arrival. It is a loving gesture and one Marv looks forward to and appreciates. Marv always buys a special gift and sends it to Vicki.

This year at Million Dollar Round Table Marv asked some of his friends if they had sent anything to their wives yet. They did not understand what he was even talking about. Why should we send something to our wives? Marv said, "Because you're in San Francisco and they're at home." He took them to Tiffany's and they each sent a little some-thing home to their wives. One of the agents called Marv as soon as he got home to thank him for saving his life. He said his wife was so pleased he had "remembered" their anniversary while he was in San Francisco! Saved!

## 🍀 Jerry and Melody Figurski

Jerry and Melody do not consider themselves a "touchy-feely" couple. Melody says she is even less "touchy-feely" than Jerry is. But, as far as "Kisses, Hugs, and More" they share a lot!

Melody claims that Jerry is the most caring, most expressive husband any woman could ask for. He is constantly showing his love for her in different ways. If she is stressed, he is always there for her. He is never short on praise for her. He sends her beautiful cards. He writes her loving notes and letters. Melody says he does this far more often and far better than she does. He expresses his love and affection exquisitely. He also sends flowers and brings her gifts to express his love.

Jerry says Melody underestimates her own shows of affection. She does it differently than he does, yes, but she does it in her own way. She does not shower him with cards, notes and letters. She showers him with her "glow," her smiles, and her words of encouragement. She is not the type to fawn all over him, but he says her unbelievable energy and efforts are unyielding in caring for him, their children, and everyone else she loves. She has always encouraged him in all of his pursuits and praised him for his accomplishments. Her smile alone says, "I love you."

Melody's "Kisses, Hugs, and More" had the same positive effect on their children as it had on Jerry. Melody spent so many hours tending to Tracy's many needs. Her love and devotion to Tracy, always talking and working with her, contributed to Tracy's upbeat, happy nature. The same is true with their son, David. Her undying energy and devotion helped David become the well adjusted, intelligent, caring young man he is today.

There is no better example of Jerry's "Kisses, Hugs, and More" than during Melody's bout with cancer. Going through the surgery and chemo was a difficult time made much easier by Jerry's incredible thoughtfulness. Jerry, along with Melody's mom, was at every chemotherapy session. He would have a little "chemo gift" ready for her the day after the treatment. It might be a bottle of perfume or a pair of earrings. He also came up with a very special, uplifting idea. He arranged to have someone from her past (usually a college friend) call her the night after each treatment. It became a routine Melody really looked forward to. And, it certainly made the nine months of chemotherapy a little more bearable.

A strange incident occurred a few years before Melody had her mastectomy. Jerry would often exclaim, "Woo Woo" when observing Melody undressing or in the shower. On this particular day after Jerry made one of his "Woo Woo" exclamations Melody asked him what would happen if she had to have a mastectomy. He said, "I guess I would have to say just, 'Woo'." The day after her surgery she received a dozen roses with a note attached saying, "No matter what, "Woo Woo!"

Jerry and Melody, although not the "touchy-feely" types, are continually sharing "Kisses, Hugs, and More." Their love and dedication to each other is very apparent.

## 🍀 Joe and Harriet Coren

Joe and Harriet have always been a very caring, loving, thoughtful, and devoted couple. From their very first date until today Joe opens the car door for Harriet. Joe is extremely kind and considerate. Harriet really appreciates it.

Joe also takes the time to do special little things for Harriet. One humorous example of this was when Harriet was "in jail" soliciting bail money for Muscular Dystrophy. Before Joe went to pick her up he packed her a cupcake with a little saw and wrapped it in paper with black bars on it. He is not naturally the artistic type so the effort was even more meaningful. Harriet still has the wrapping paper.

After 53 years of marriage Joe and Harriet make sure to kiss each morning and each evening. If one of them goes to bed before the other they make sure to kiss the sleeping spouse.

Harriet is still working and Joe is now a retired "house husband." He will stop into Harriet's office and ask what she would like for dinner. Joe also does all the shopping. Harriet says this is a wonderful example of "Kisses, Hugs, and More." His consideration and effort allows her to freely pursue her work tasks.

## 💔 John Green and Susan Capio

"Kisses, Hugs, and More" are definitely limited these days for John and Susan. Juggling careers, children, and couple time is very challenging—a delicate balance to try to maintain. Instead of the individual and couple activities they did for so many years before having children, most of their time is now spent participating in activities they can enjoy as a family (movies, amusement parks, nature walks, museums, sports, Broadway shows, etc.)

John and Susan try to kiss each morning before they part and every evening before they go to sleep. Hugs are very limited these days—the girls are always there to squeeze in. At six and three years old, they are definitely "daddy's girls," not willing to share dad's hugs with each other or with mom. John and Susan are drawing further apart. To save their relationship they must find time to share "Kisses, Hugs and More" before it is too late!

"Kisses, Hugs, and More" are so important in a marriage. You might not spray the rose petals and have the best champagne like when you were dating, but it is important to keep the relationship alive. This is especially true in the years when business and children are your main focus. Do not lose the connection with your mate. Do this for your spouse. Do this for yourself. Do this for your children.

Here is a checklist for the "K":

113

## CHECKLIST FOR THE "K"

___ 1. **MAKE TIME FOR
LOVEMAKING.**

___ 2. **SHARE KISSES
AND HUGS.**

___ 3. **HOLD HANDS
AND CONNECT.**

___ 4. **SHOW YOU CARE WITH A
SMILE, A WINK, OR A
LOOK OF APPROVAL.**

___ 5. **ALWAYS TRY TO BE THERE
FOR YOUR SPOUSE.**

\_\_ 6. **SHOW YOU CARE ABOUT YOUR SPOUSE'S FEELINGS.**

\_\_ 7. **TRY NOT TO CRITICIZE YOUR SPOUSE.**

\_\_ 8. **GIVE PRAISE AND COMPLIMENTS TO YOUR SPOUSE AS OFTEN AS YOU CAN.**

\_\_ 9. **BUY SPECIAL GIFTS.**

\_\_ 10. **COOK A SPECIAL MEAL.**

\_\_ 11. **WRITE A LOVING NOTE. SEND A CARD.**

__ 12.  **DO A CHORE WITHOUT
BEING ASKED.**

__ 13.  **LISTEN TO AND EMPATHIZE
WITH YOUR SPOUSE.**

__ 14.  **SAY, "I LOVE YOU."**

# CHAPTER FIVE

## "Y"

## "Y" Stands for YOU

The first letter in a "L.U.C.K.Y." marriage is the "L" which stands for "Like." Like is the first and most important ingredient in a "lucky" marriage, but it is the last letter, "Y" where the buck stops. The last letter is for YOU. YOU are the key factor in a "lucky" marriage. YOU are the one who makes it "lucky." YOU must take responsibility for the successes in your life. YOU must take responsibility for your marriage.

The first responsibility is to choose a partner who is right for you. This must be a person with whom you plan to spend the rest of your life. Once you have made that decision and it is your "final answer," you are the one who must put every effort into making the marriage work. Of course, there are two of you; and it is the two of you that together must make it work.

117

## WHAT TO LOOK FOR IN A SPOUSE

What should you look for in a spouse? Many young people dissect this question today. More thought and effort is put into this decision perhaps because of the record number of failed marriages in the last few decades. Many have seen, heard, and in some cases, experienced the horrors resulting from divorce, or from years of staying together in an unhappy marriage. Young people do not want to make the same mistakes their parents made. Caution has led many individuals to wait until they are much older to marry or to decide not to marry at all. Until we see the divorce statistics over the next decade or two, it is impossible to determine whether the new tendency toward caution is good or not.

So what should you look for in a mate? Start by looking for someone you like. As discussed at length in Chapter One liking the person you marry has a tremendous effect on the "luck" of your marriage. In Chapter Two we discussed many areas of unity— goals, values, religion, family, environment, etc. The more areas of unity the better your chance for a "lucky" marriage. Common interests are also important. How wonderful to marry someone with whom you share many interests. It makes for a much more binding relationship when you both have a passion for some special activity or activities. Remember though—interests can be developed if "like" and "unity" in other areas are strong.

Another major factor that may affect the relationship of a couple is their behavioral styles. We all have different styles of behaving. Our behavioral styles define our individual ways of dealing with situations and people. How we view things, our emotions, our fears, our goals, our strengths, and our limitations are a result of our behavioral styles. What style are you? What style individual is right for you? What style should you look for in a mate? What styles make the best combinations? Is there a combination of styles that are best suited for each other? Are there combinations that are not suited for each other? Are there some styles that if united would be a major disaster? Is there one perfect style to match your style? There are no bad styles, just different styles. Let's explore all the possibilities.

## DISC BEHAVIORAL STYLES

The DISC Behavioral Styles help us understand ourselves and others. The DISC Styles are not used to label or box people, but rather to create awareness. Each individual is truly unique and special. When I conduct my training programs I relate learning the basic DISC Styles to learning basic colors or numbers. You need to know the basics before you understand the combinations. There are four main Styles—Dominance, Influencing, Steadiness and Conscientiousness. Each individual is a combination of these four styles. Each possesses different levels of the various styles. Some are very high in one style and not so high in another.

Dominance is the first of the four DISC Styles. A dominant person is direct, take charge, and decisive. This type of individual likes to control situations. He or she fears loss of control. They are no nonsense, get the job done people who are very task oriented. Their main attention is focused on the task at hand. They are quick to move and fast to take action. Routine can lead to boredom and discontentment. They are fast paced individuals who thrive on change and challenge.

The second style is Influencing. The influencing person is an upbeat, fun-loving, enthusiastic individual. The influencing person thrives on being loved and accepted by others. The Influencing style individual fears rejection. This is the kind of person who tries to keep everybody happy. Their main attention is focused on people. They are great at building enthusiasm within the group. They are fast paced individuals who thrive on being with people. They love a fast moving environment with many people related activities.

The third style is the Steadiness style. The steadiness person is steady, sincere, and supportive. The Steadiness style needs to exist in a comfortable, familiar environment. This style individual fears change. The steady individual enjoys an environment where everything is calm and proceeds as expected. Routine is comforting. Their main focus is on people. They move at a slow, steady pace. They are wonderful team players.

The fourth style is the Conscientiousness style. The conscientiousness person is precise, detailed, and thorough. The Conscientiousness style has a strong drive for correctness. Conscientious individuals seek perfection and therefore fear being criticized. They need an environment where they have the time and ability to get things done completely and correctly. They definitely are task oriented. They thrive on the opportunity to get projects done individually, correctly, and at their own pace. They move slowly and deliberately.

For more style awareness let's take a look at the major differences:

## FAST PACED

Dominance

Influencing

## SLOW PACED

Steadiness

Conscientiousness

## PEOPLE ORIENTED

Influencing

Steadiness

## TASK ORIENTED

Dominance

Conscientiousness

## D: DOMINANCE

**FAST PACED
TASK ORIENTED**

Decisive

Independent

Efficient

Competitive

Direct

*To get along most effectively
with the Dominant style:*

*Be brief!*

*Be bright!*

*Be gone!*

I:   **INFLUENCING**

**FAST PACED**
**PEOPLE ORIENTED**

Enthusiastic

Stimulating

Persuasive

Optimistic

Talkative

*To get along most effectively*
*with the Influencing style:*

Be fast!

Be fun!

Be flexible!

## S: STEADINESS

## SLOW PACED
## PEOPLE ORIENTED

Trusting

Dependable

Agreeable

Stable

Supportive

*To get along most effectively
with the Steadiness style:*

Be steady!

Be sincere!

Be supportive!

## C: CONSCIENTIOUSNESS

**SLOW PACED
TASK ORIENTED**

Accurate

Detailed

Sensitive

Persistent

Cautious

*To get along most effectively
with the Conscientiousness style:*

Be precise!

Be detailed!

Be thorough!

There you have a quick overview of the four styles.

What combination of styles would make a "lucky" marriage? Any combination of styles can have meaningful, successful relationships. All combinations of styles can be united to form a "lucky" marriage. The key to the ultimate success of any relationship is understanding, acceptance, and appreciation of each other's styles.

Let's take a look at the DISC profiles of the couples used in the book:

## 🍀Siracusa

| Pat | Judy |
|---|---|
| I | IS |
| FAST PACED | FAST PACED |
| PEOPLE ORIENTED | PEOPLE ORIENTED |

## 🍀Feldman

| Marv | Vicki |
|---|---|
| C | C |
| SLOW PACED | SLOW PACED |
| TASK ORIENTED | TASK ORIENTED |

## 🍀 Figurski

| Jerry | Melody |
|---|---|
| DI | I |
| FAST PACED | FAST PACED |
| TASK ORIENTED | PEOPLE ORIENTED |

## 🍀Coren

| Joe | Harriet |
|---|---|
| S | DC |
| SLOW PACED | FAST PACED |
| PEOPLE ORIENTED | TASK ORIENTED |

## 💔 Green/Capio

| John | Susan |
|---|---|
| CD | ID |
| SLOW PACED | FAST PACED |
| TASK ORIENTED | PEOPLE ORIENTED |

## ♣ Pat and Judy Siracusa I/IS

Pat and I have very similar profiles. The Influencing style is the highest style for both of us. Pat does not have a second high style. His other three styles are fairly even with none of them high enough to be factored into his profile. The Influencing style as the main high style is called the Promoter Pattern. My second style is the Steadiness style. The combination of my two styles, Influencing and Steadiness, is called the Counselor Pattern. This pattern is very people oriented. Let's look at how our similar styles affect our relationship.

We are both FAST PACED. This is great for us as a couple. We both have incredible energy levels. We are constantly on the go! And we both like it that way! Pat has more energy than anyone I know. Married to a less energized person, Pat would have to find many more things to do on his own. As it is, we both love to have many different, varied activities in our lives. We both thrive on fun and adventure. Most of our friends have trouble keeping up with us. Even our children and their wives say we tire them out!

A normal weekend for us may start by meeting at home on Friday at 2:00 p.m., changing and being out on the first tee by 2:30 p.m., playing 18 holes of golf, finishing by 6:30 p.m., showering, changing and meeting friends for dinner by 7:15 p.m. The Saturday schedule may include some tennis, watching a college football game, and finally dinner with friends, or a fund-raiser cocktail party, or a dinner dance of some nature. Sunday we may ride our bikes to church, then continue out to the beach, have brunch, and ride home (about a 20-mile stretch).  Sunday at 5:00 p.m. our family comes over for a traditional Italian Sunday dinner that I prepare.  There are usually seven or more in attendance—our three sons, two daughters-in-law, plus Grandma, plus any cousins or friends in from out of town.

We are both PEOPLE ORIENTED.  We love people.  We have maintained many long time friendships.  And, we are always meeting and making new friends.  We are also very close to our families.  Our love of young people is one reason we both enjoyed teaching so much.  In fact, each field we have pursued through the years has been people-oriented.  Pat succeeded in the tennis business because of his incredible ability to work with people, many of whom are still our very good friends and some of Pat's best clients.

Neither Pat nor I are particularly materialistic.  We have a nice, comfortable home and two nice, conservatively priced cars.  Our home is stylishly furnished, but not with excessively expensive things.  We try to dress well without buying outlandishly expensive clothes.  I love jewelry, but costume jewelry is fine with me.  We would rather spend our money traveling to see family and friends, going on unique vacations, or purchasing equipment for our sporting activities.

The Conscientiousness style is both of our lowest styles.  Attending to details, therefore, is not one of our strengths.  This could be a problem if neither of us took the initiative to take charge of bills and records, and other detailed necessities.  Pat may not like it, but he does all this and does it well.  Sometimes you have to discipline yourself to do things that are not favorite tasks, but which are necessary and important. We both have strong work ethics and are very responsible individuals. In business we also take the extra time and effort to keep our records and other important data updated and in order.

As a financial planner, Pat knows that his greatest strength is his ability to work with his clients, so he has surrounded himself with a conscientious support team. They take care of making sure all the paperwork and details are meticulously prepared. This allows him more time to spend with his clients. In my business, I always prepare far ahead of time, arriving at my keynotes and training sessions very early. This is my defense against being unprepared. I always have time to make adjustments, if necessary. Pat teases me about arriving so far in advance, however, we each find our own ways to compensate for our limitations.

The necessity of acquiring detailed information and research is not a high priority with us. It is very obvious when we are shopping for a car or appliances for our home. We have been known to go into a store and purchase a new stove or dishwasher in less than ten minutes. This is not an exaggeration! Because we both like to function this way—it works. I cannot imagine being married to a spouse who analyzes and compares everything. It would truly drive me crazy. When we go shopping for clothes it is an "in and out" adventure. We try, we buy, and we leave.

Our very similar styles work for us. We enjoy our fast paced lives and our active involvement with many people.

Our lack of conscientiousness and difficulty focusing on details has not been a major problem. I guess this is because Pat has enough common sense to take charge of the bills and the checkbooks. We love our very active lives and have enjoyed our "lucky" marriage for over 35 years.

## 🍀 Marvin and Vicki Feldman C/C

Marv and Vicki have practically identical behavioral profiles. Their highest style is the C—Conscientiousness style. And, similarly, neither of them have a second style that is high enough to effect their profiles. The conscientious individual is very cautious, very analytical and very precise in everything they do. Marv and Vicki's life experiences shared throughout this book clearly exemplify that they do things with preparation and forethought. They are both slow paced and task oriented.

Having the same styles works wonderfully for them. It could be challenging for two other individuals with the same "C" styles. Conflict could arise when they each decide on the correct way to do something and it is different from the way the other one thinks it should be done. Remember the "C" style's main goal is correctness and their greatest fear is criticism. So, when two conscientious people do not agree about the way things should be done, there could be a lot of conflict. Marv and Vicki do not have these conflicts. One reason is because they respect each other's ability to do things correctly.

They take on many projects together while splitting the responsibilities of certain other tasks between them. Setting goals and planning their future has always been done together with care and precision. Family goals, financial goals, and goals for fun and relaxation were systematically established before they married.

They retain their separate domains of control. Vicki's is the kitchen. In the kitchen things are done her way. She has her system and Marv goes with the system. He, on the other hand, is in charge of washing the cars. Marv does not take his cars to the car wash. There is only one way to wash Marv's cars . . . Marv's way! Vicki often helps with washing the car. She knows Marv's system and follows it.

They also make major purchases together—using a system. They both love to shop. They research and analyze things carefully before deciding exactly what to buy. In fact, shopping and negotiating are more exciting for Marv than the actual purchase. Once he has researched, shopped, negotiated, and finally purchased the item the fun is over . . . until the next purchase! Marv is so good at shopping and negotiating that his friends and acquaintances call upon him often to do it for them. His gun club always requests Marv to shop and purchase the competition pistols for them.

Before starting the search for a new car Marv researches all the available information—including data on the Internet. By the time he sets out on his quest he knows

133

all there is to know about the vehicles—even more than most sales people he deals with!

List making is a routine activity for Marv and Vicki. They make lots of lists! Each make lists, then compare and analyze what is on their respective lists. Building their homes were full time projects. It took two years to build their first home. They looked at plans separately, picked plans individually, then compared and analyzed the plans together. After exploring all the options they selected their final plans. It was a long, tedious process. For them it was a labor of love.

Marv and Vicki prepare for social occasions with the same intensity some people prepare for a test. When traveling to a new area or a foreign country they thoroughly research the culture. They will spend hours before a trip at Barnes and Noble reading about the land, the customs, the protocol, and any other information that will help them feel more comfortable in the group. Preparing for a social event is hard work for them, but it is worth the effort not to be put in an uncomfortable social situation.

Their conscientious natures and sound decision making abilities are a blessing when difficult family situations need to be handled. When Vicki's aunt was ill and had to be hospitalized Marv and Vicki were called upon to make the final plans. Family and friends rely on them because everyone is confident in Marv and Vicki's ability to analyze options and come up with the best solutions.

134

Their Conscientiousness styles have also been useful where Marv's health is concerned. Marv has been challenged by diabetes over the past few years. The proactive stance Marv has taken in dealing with the disease has paid off. When he was first diagnosed Marv and Vicki went together to the bookstore and to classes to educate themselves. They have continued to intensely research everything to learn and understand as much as possible about the condition. Due to indepth research they learned to control his diabetes by changing their eating habits. At first, diet and exercise were enough to control it, now medication is also necessary. Marv not only researched data about diabetes, he researched the doctors in the field. Knowing more than most doctors, he settled on a specialist in California. Now Marv assists doctors in his local area by providing contacts and information.

As their girls were growing up, Marv and Vicki always required them to perform to the best of their abilities. Some high "C's" can be too demanding of perfection from their children. Some are extremely critical. Expecting and accepting nothing but perfection at all times is too challenging even for the most exceptional children. Marv and Vicki, fortunately, were not like that. They did not demand perfection, only that their girls did the best they could. Marv and Vicki were very positive and complimentary of Terri and Barbi. They have become two lovely, self-confident, independent young women.

Marv and Vicki are so compatible and so much alike. Yes, they are both perfectionists who thrive on doing things correctly. They are also positive, upbeat individuals who like, love, and respect each other with all their hearts!

## 🍀 Jerry and Melody Figurski DI/I

Jerry and Melody have different highest styles, but they both have the Influencing style as a major part of their profiles. Jerry's highest style is the Dominant style, which makes him fast paced and task oriented. Melody's highest style is the Influencing style, which makes her also fast paced. However, her first focus is on people. She is always "thinking" and "doing" for others.

They are both very high-energy individuals. They thrive on being on the go. Finding time to do everything on their schedules would be a challenge for most people. Not them! If their plates were not totally full they would feel unfulfilled. It is this high energy level that allows them to maintain business and family commitments, still having time for all their community volunteerism and participation in their many fun activities and interests.

Dominant styles sometimes tend to aggressively jump into situations. Jerry has been known to do this. Melody tends to be more reluctant to jump. She is more cautious. When they face difficult situations, Jerry forges ahead convinced things will turn out all right. The problem Jerry has is not taking on challenges, but rather dealing with the results when they do not come out the way he plans. Melody may be more emotional, but she is better at accepting things as they are. Jerry is more optimistic and determined during a crisis, but he has greater difficulty accepting a bad result. When they found out that Tracy was both physically and mentally disabled it was devastating for both of them. Yet, it was harder for Jerry because he felt somehow defective in not being able to do something to change the outcome.

Their styles have complemented each other beautifully through all their major challenges. Balancing their styles helped them survive and grow through the bad times and allowed them to enjoy the good times.

## 🍀 Joe and Harriet Coren  S/DC

Joe and Harriet have very different profiles. They have few similarities in their styles. Their first two styles: "S" and "D" are diametrical opposites! Joe's Steadiness style is slow paced and people oriented. Harriet's Dominant style is fast paced and task oriented. Joe's Steadiness style makes him a calm, sincere man who is comfortable in an environment where things remain constant. Change is a challenge for Joe. Harriet's Dominant style not only allows her to make changes easily, but she actually thrives on change and variety in her life. When things remain too routine she gets bored. She is always searching for new adventures. She loves to be in charge. She loves to make decisions.

How do they deal with their extreme differences? They deal with them quite well. Harriet likes to take charge—and so she does. Joe is a supportive team player and so he plays by Harriet's rules—most of the time. Harriet is fast paced and, at the age of 73, she is still working and moving in many directions. Joe joins her at his own pace when he can and when she asks him. They have a great working relationship. Sure, at times Harriet might get frustrated with Joe's apparent lack of quickness and decisiveness and Joe, in turn, might get exhausted and frustrated by Harriet's aggressive nature. But, you just have to meet them to see that there is so much respect and appreciation between the two of them. Harriet has been the captain of their "lucky" team and Joe the willing player for over 53 years. It works for them.

##  John Green and Susan Capio CD/ID

John and Susan's main styles are quite different. John's primary style is a C—Conscientiousness. The "C" style is slow paced and task oriented. Susan's highest style is an I—Influencing, which is just the opposite—fast paced and people oriented. John's second style is D—Dominant which is also opposite of his own first style. The "D" style is fast paced and task oriented. John's "CD" combination can be conflicting even within him. His combination of styles is called the Creative Pattern. The Creative Pattern makes him appear to be low key, but in many ways he is definitely not low key. He is actually quite demanding of himself and others. The creative person likes things done totally and completely correctly, yet also quickly. This can cause challenges and conflict. Susan's "I" and "D" styles are practically even. This combination is called the Inspirational Pattern. She is fast paced and both people and task oriented. She quickly takes control of things with charm and enthusiasm.

Their different styles could be effective in keeping John and Susan in balance as individuals and as a couple. Susan could give John the convincing push he needs to nudge him out of his comfort zone to reach for his goals, while John could supply Susan with the stability and comfort she sometimes needs. The combination could work very much like Joe and Harriet's combination. Opposite styles work great for them.

Unfortunately, John and Susan have started to butt heads more often when their styles conflict during normal day-to-day decision making. Susan thinks John procrastinates too much. John fears rushing into things before he is totally comfortable and prepared. He analyzes all possibilities before making a decision, hating to make the wrong decision. He hates to fail! Susan, on the other hand, makes decisions with a leap of faith without fear or anxiety—assuming it will all work out. Sometimes they come together on their decisions but lately they are in conflict more often than not. To work together more effectively, John will need to systematically take a few more risks and Susan will have to take a little more time to analyze risks before jumping into things.

They could draw tremendous strength from their different styles as do Joe and Harriet. John and Susan have done this in the past. John always made the purchases for their home. He researched, shopped, and checked out all the options. After analyzing it all, he made the best choices. John has the patience for that. Susan does not. Susan, on the other hand, has always been strong in the big money decision process. In many ways their different styles could be a bigger asset than a limitation.

A recent challenge came during Susan's last promotion that prompted their move back down south. Susan was offered a new position and, in her natural style, jumped into action moving forward with the plans. John, although he wanted to move back, found it difficult to make such a fast transition. John contemplates. Susan plunges!

John and Susan have very different high styles. These differences, although challenging at times, could help more than hinder them. They could draw strength from each other. John and Susan need to make an effort to understand each other better. They need to appreciate and respect their individual strengths and limitations. They did in the beginning.

The styles of the four "lucky" couples represented in this book are very different from each other. Some of the "lucky" couples share very similar styles with their partners, while others have totally opposite styles. Yet each of the "lucky" couples have achieved a high level of success in their married lives.

The fifth couple, John and Susan, who are presently struggling with their marriage, have different styles. It is not their style differences that are the cause of their marital problems. Joe and Harriet have extremely different styles and it has worked for them for over 53 years! At the beginning of their relationship these differences also worked well for John and Susan. Having children is not what is ruining their marriage. Having children has forced their lack of common interests, lack of time together, and limited communication to develop into major problems in their relationship. Their goals and dreams also changed following the birth of their children. This often happens. Unfortunately for John and Susan these changes did not develop in unison. John and Susan can still save their marriage. However, they need to make a serious commitment to rebuilding their relationship. They must make the time and effort to re-establish their goals and dreams. They need to reorganize their lives in order to fulfill both their couple needs as well as the needs of their family. It will not be easy. They have let their differences separate them, frustrate them, and alienate them. They have so much to save. I hope they make the effort.

In conclusion, it is not whether a couple shares similar styles or different styles that is important. What is important is how well a couple learns to work with their partner's style. Different styles can get along. Similar styles can get along. It all goes back to understanding, acceptance, and appreciation!

Here is the checklist for the "Y":

# CHECKLIST FOR THE "Y"

__ 1. There are no bad styles.

__ 2. Everyone is a combination of all styles—stronger in some than in others.

__ 3. All style combinations can have a "lucky" marriage.

__4. Learn to know, understand, and appreciate your own strengths and limitations.

__5. Learn to know, understand, and appreciate your spouse's strengths and limitations.

__6. Use your combined strengths to develop your "lucky" marriage.

## CONCLUSION

"Lucky" marriages don't just happen! There are reasons for the "luck" in a "lucky" marriage. There are some qualities and beliefs necessary for marriages to be more than mundane and frustrating unions.

"Like" is the first necessary ingredient. Liking your spouse makes the life challenges that are sure to come along much easier to deal with.

"Unity" will help strengthen a marriage. Some areas of unity are necessities; other areas are pluses that will enhance the enjoyment and closeness of a couple. Unity of spirit, commitment, and goals are necessities. Unity of interests, pets, environment, and religion are pluses. The biggest decision and greatest commitment made by a couple is to have or not to have children. This decision must be made as a couple.

"Communication" must be strong and effective to maintain a "lucky" marriage.

"Kisses, Hugs, and More" are needed to keep the relationship fun and alive. In order for a marriage to be "lucky" there must be some form of "Kisses, Hugs, and More." Each "lucky" couple does this in their own diverse way. But, they are necessary to keep a marriage stimulating.

"YOU" are the most important ingredient in a "lucky" marriage. "YOU" as an individual with all your behavioral strengths and limitations must make the commitment to understand and appreciate your spouse's strengths and limitations.

Yes, "L.U.C.K.Y." marriages don't just happen! That is why it is so important to understand the ingredients that go into having a "lucky" marriage! Remember marriage can be the WORST or the BEST! BEST is better!

# BACKGROUNDS OF THE COUPLES

## 🍀 Pat and Judy Siracusa

Pat and Judy met in 1961 as freshmen at the University of New York, College at Cortland. They were both Physical Education majors. After dating all four years of college they married two weeks following graduation and have been married for over 35 years. They have three sons, Pat, Jr., David and Brian. Pat, Jr. is a prosecutor and his wife, Kara, is director of marketing for an Internet company. David is a financial planner and his wife, Fran, is a high school Spanish teacher. Brian is pursuing a career in sports broadcasting.

Pat is a financial planner with AXA Advisors. Judy has her own business, WINNING WAYS of Tampa Bay, Inc., a speaking and training corporation. They have lived in the Tampa Bay area of Florida for over 26 years.

## 🍀 Marvin and Vicki Feldman

Marv and Vicki have been married for over 34 years. They grew up and went all through school together in their home-town of East Liverpool, Ohio. They met in second grade and married after Marv graduated from college. They have two grown daughters, Terri and Barbi. Terri is an attorney by education, presently working in the film industry as the president of a small production company in California. She will be married this year to Rick Lubaroff.  Barbi is an attorney married to David Meyer, who is also an attorney.  They live on the east coast of Florida.

Marv Feldman has been with New York Life and at the top of the insurance industry for years!  He will be the President of Million Dollar Round Table in 2002.  Vicki is wife, mother, and full-family caretaker.

## 🍀 Jerry and Melody Figurski

Jerry and Melody met at Kent State and have been married for over 33 years.  They are very well known in the Tampa Bay area of Florida for their extensive community volunteerism.  Together they have conquered numerous challenges, including having a mentally and physically disabled daughter and Melody's fight against breast cancer eight years ago.  Melody has had her picture and name added to the Football Hall of Fame in Canton, Ohio as the "Ultimate Buccaneer Fan."

They have two children.  Tracy is presently living in a UPARC group home in the Tampa Bay area.  David is married.  He and his wife, Melissa, graduated with degrees in civil engineering from the University of Florida and are presently in graduate school at the University of Texas.

Jerry is a very successful partner in a law firm in Tampa Bay.  Melody is a fully committed community volunteer.

## 🍀 Joe and Harriet Coren

Joe and Harriet met in 1945 at a dance for returning service men. They had both already graduated from high school and were in the process of developing their individual careers. Joe worked in his family business, the food and beverage industry, and Harriet had started her long career as a secretary. She spent many years working in the insurance industry with Equitable Life and also assisted a number of successful authors editing and publishing books. Joe is retired. Harriet still runs her own secretarial business and is the Director of Administrative Services of Leadership Pinellas.

They have two children. Susie is an occupational therapist, married to Ken Shear and parents of Joe and Harriet's grandchildren, Adena and Yoni. Buzz is a craftsman, married to silk screen artist, Debbie. They are the parents of Joe and Harriet's newest long-awaited grandchild, little Sophia, recently adopted from China.

Joe and Harriet reside in Palm Harbor, Florida. Their "lucky" marriage has been going strong for over 53 years.

## 💔 John Green and Susan Capio

John and Susan married in 1987 after meeting on a blind date in 1982. John graduated from Boston University with a BS in Accounting. He received his MBA at the University of South Florida. Susan also graduated from Boston University with a BS in Education.

They live in Florida with their two young daughters, Michelle and Jennifer.  John's profession is in medical sales.  Susan is the only female president of the medical company she represents.  She is president of the entire southeastern region.

# APPENDIX

Do you know your style?

Do you know your spouse
or potential spouse's style?

Want to find out your style?

Want to find out your spouse
or potential spouse's style?

Want to know, understand, and
appreciate yourself better?

Want to know, understand,
and appreciate your spouse
or potential spouse better?

Get a complete personal profile
report all about YOU!


Just complete a 28 question profile
answer sheet in ten short minutes


Receive a complete
computer printout report
with a minimum of 18 pages

or


Receive a more complete
comprehensive report of
up to 125 pages

To order a report, please contact:

---

**Judy Siracusa**
**WINNING WAYS of Tampa Bay, Inc.**
**1212 4th Ave. SW**
**Largo, FL  33770**

> **or**

**phone:  727-518-6555**

**fax:     727-518-2002**

**Email:   winningwaystampa@msn.com**

---

**Help yourself have a "lucky" marriage.**
**Get your personal profile report today.**

**Remember**
**"L.U.C.K.Y." Marriages**
**Don't Just Happen!**